WHEN PEOPLE RISE

HR SECRETS FOR SMALL BUSINESS GROWTH, SUCCESS, AND LEGACY

SUSAN S. MAHAFFEE

HEATHER ARCHER · EMILY OWENS CHANNELL · JAIME DAMKROGER
AGNES GEISLER · ELIZABETH HARRIS · ADINA M. LAVOIE · BEN MADDEN
SABINA MAY · RICK MILLER · SONIA E. PACHECO · SANITA PINCHBACK
DR. PAMELA J. PINE · STACEY PIPER · LAURA REYNOLDS
JILL A. ROGERS · SHELLY SCHOFF · AISHA SCOTT · KRIS VALERIO SHOCK
MAURA DOWD SNIEGOSKI · KATIE L. TANNER · BROOKE TOOMEY

WHEN PEOPLE RISE

HR SECRETS FOR SMALL BUSINESS GROWTH, SUCCESS, AND LEGACY

SUSAN S. MAHAFFEE

HEATHER ARCHER · EMILY OWENS CHANNELL · JAIME DAMKROGER
AGNES GEISLER · ELIZABETH HARRIS · ADINA M. LAVOIE · BEN MADDEN
SABINA MAY · RICK MILLER · SONIA E. PACHECO · SANITA PINCHBACK
DR. PAMELA J. PINE · STACEY PIPER · LAURA REYNOLDS
JILL A. ROGERS · SHELLY SCHOFF · AISHA SCOTT · KRIS VALERIO SHOCK
MAURA DOWD SNIEGOSKI · KATIE L. TANNER · BROOKE TOOMEY

"Filled with great storytelling and a bevy of unique perspectives, *When People Rise* is the people-centered handbook all leaders and HR professionals need to read."

- Andrew Biernat

Author of *The Team That Loves Mondays*, Team Transformation Expert, Curator of the HR.Salon Community and Host of the HR.Salon Podcast

---

"As the founder of a business and employment law firm, I see firsthand how often companies underestimate the impact of their people strategy—until it becomes a legal or operational issue. Susan's book, *When People Rise*, is a refreshing and much-needed shift from reactive thinking to intentional leadership."

- Francisco Mundaca

Founding Partner, The Mundaca Law Firm

"I truly appreciate how *When People Rise* highlights practical, intentional, and straightforward actions that help shape stronger, more impactful leaders. By focusing on easy-to-apply strategies, the book encourages genuine growth and makes leadership accessible to all. It's an inspiring guide for anyone who wants to make a difference and rise together with their teams."

- Lauren Gaul

Senior Vice President, People and Culture, Dancker

"Susan and her coauthors remind us of the imperative of the 'human' in Human Resources. This book teaches us how to invest in our people relationships and navigate the complex yet beautiful way humans drive our businesses and are the real key to success. As a CEO of a nonprofit organization, I found this book extremely powerful, with both the heartfelt stories that I can connect with and the tools I am already putting into practice."

- Julie Campbell

CEO, Severn Leadership Group

"As a new leader and CEO, *When People Rise* has inspired a new confidence in me - empowering me to turn uncertainty and self-doubt into opportunity. The practical insights and heartfelt stories are a powerful reminder of the impact of genuine community connection and that we never have to lead alone."

- Amy Berry

CEO, Anne Arundel County Chamber of Commerce (Maryland)

"An enjoyable collection of stories from HR experts and business owners who present challenging situations that they resolve through practical wisdom and human warmth. A great read for anyone who works with people, which is everyone!"

- Liz League

CEO, Greater Severna Park and Arnold Chamber of Commerce

"A must-read for any HR leader who has ever felt the weight of a difficult conversation. The book's true superpower is its ability to make the tough conversations more meaningful and less menacing."

- Lance Young, Ed.D., pHCLE,

Chief Human Resources Officer, Walton County School District, Georgia

---

DEDICATION

**This book is dedicated to my son,
Peter Bank Joseph Mahaffee.**

*I hope one day you'll see not just what I built,
but the values behind it —
that leading with humanity, care,
and respect for people is not separate from success,
but the path to it.*

You carry forward a legacy that inspired me first.

DISCLAIMER

This book is intended to offer thoughtful, reliable guidance on human resources, people leadership, and the real-world challenges of building better workplaces. However, it is sold with the understanding that the authors and publisher specifically disclaim all responsibility for any liability, loss, or risk, personal or otherwise, incurred as a consequence, directly or indirectly, of the use and application of any of the contents of this publication.

In order to maintain the anonymity of others, the names and identifying characteristics of some people, places, and organizations described in this book have been changed.

Our authors represent cultures worldwide, and as such, there may be differences in language and expressions. As a global publisher, we have made the conscious choice not to edit these nuances, so each chapter is authentic and in its author's words.

Know that the experts here have shared their tools, practices, and knowledge with you with a sincere and generous intent to assist you on your personal journey. Please contact them with any questions you may have about the techniques or information they provided. They will be happy to assist you further and be an ongoing resource for your success!

TABLE OF CONTENTS

FOREWORD

"Susan, where did you get this fantastic navy blue wallpaper?"

I can still remember yelling that question through the half-bath door while Susan was in the kitchen, multitasking with the effortless grace she always seems to display. If you could have heard her detailed explanation of the wallpaper selection, you would quickly understand that Susan reserves her time and passion for the things she loves most.

What I later discovered is that Susan is even better at choosing people than she is at choosing wallpaper. She finds profound meaning in everything, but especially in the people who surround her.

As the Fire Chief leading one of the largest fire departments in the country, Susan's perspective on the value of people deeply resonates with me. She understands that people are the most important component of any successful endeavor. My challenges as a Fire Chief are not simply the operations of extinguishing structure fires, cutting vehicles to rescue occupants, or providing CPR during life-saving medical interventions. My primary challenge is managing my most precious resource: *my people*.

I have the honor of taking care of over 1,500 personnel, along with hundreds of administrative volunteers, civilian support staff, and 911 dispatchers. Our collective challenge lies in protecting over 600,000 people who live in my community, because if I don't take care of my people, they won't be ready to take care of others. I live and breathe a profession that requires life and death decisions. I have to be able to trust the decisions of my people and their trained instincts.

What you'll find in the following pages of this book are complex lessons made simple. The authors are sharing secrets gained from having "been caught in the flames" and knowing how to extinguish problems with minimal damage.

Humor aside, this book is for EVERYONE, because everyone needs to understand that people matter in every role. It doesn't matter if you are leading 10,000 people or simply figuring out how to lead yourself. To lead effectively and to do good business, one must first understand who they are, who they work with, and how they can serve others.

Because these co-authors also share their own personal stories, the hope is that they inspire you to take action, to consider an alternate perspective, and even validate that we all need help from others to be successful, even if the path there wasn't linear.

For Susan, nothing is more paramount than people, which is precisely why she chose a profession centered entirely on human resources. Whether you have had the honor of working for her, collaborating with her, or just been lucky enough to be around her, you know Susan is deliberate and calculated in her commitment to understanding others.

She has invested so much of herself to reach the highest levels of her profession, driven by the belief that what she wants for herself, a love for her work and for the people around her, is what she wants for everyone. I would be willing to guess that if you're reading this book, this belief may resonate with you as well.

As a Fire Chief, one of my first major challenges was modernizing our entry-level firefighter hiring process to truly invest in the organization's diversity. The people you hire *are* the culture of your organization.

While I'll spare you the procedural details, as you are likely familiar with hiring processes, my solution was to personally interview the top 150 candidates in the last step of the firefighter hiring process. Many considered this approach absurd, unrealistic, and poor time management for a senior executive. However, I believe that to shape the culture, I must first have a direct hand in selecting the people who create it.

To this day, I have found no better use of my time as a leader and Fire Chief.

I don't know of any other Fire Chief who oversees a large metropolitan fire department, interviewing candidates for entry-level positions. It makes me proud to have an early impact early on in their careers by showing new firefighters that I care and that they have value within the organization, starting from their very first day on the job.

Each author in this book finds a lesson from their own experience and demonstrates the courage to try something new in order to make an impact.

The pages ahead offer more than advice; they offer perspective from leaders who have faced real challenges and learned how to move through them.

Susan has gathered voices that remind us leadership is not about titles or authority. It is about people, trust, and the courage to grow together. If this book inspires you to lead with greater clarity, compassion, and intention, then it has done exactly what it was meant to do.

When people rise, organizations rise, we rise.

Trisha L. Wolford MBA, MS, EFO, CFO, FM, NRP

Fire Chief / President & Board Chair, IAFC

Anne Arundel County Fire Department (MD)

INTRODUCTION

This book began with a simple belief—one I've carried with me as a leader, an advisor, and a business owner: **People are never an afterthought. They are the strategy.**

I've spent my career inside organizations of all kinds—large companies, growing startups, family businesses, and everything in between. And what I've seen, time and again, is that success doesn't hinge on having the perfect plan or the most polished policies. It hinges on trust. On integrity. On how people are treated when things are hard, uncertain, or changing.

Last August, during a conversation in my Annapolis-based women's networking group, the publisher of this very book invited us to think back to an earlier time in our careers—or to the moment we first started our businesses. She asked where we went for advice, answers, and inspiration when we were figuring things out and didn't yet have a clear roadmap.

THAT QUESTION STAYED WITH ME.

I thought about being the youngest leader on executive teams, and often the only woman in the room.

Am I going to have to prove myself again today?

I thought about standing on manufacturing floors in heels during meetings, then switching into safety shoes and a hairnet to walk the line.

If I don't show up where the work happens, nothing else I say will matter.

I thought about working in the waste industry alongside men who had worked with women leaders before—but not one who showed up the way I did.

They weren't questioning my role. They were questioning whether I belonged.

I wasn't afraid to ride in a trash truck through Baltimore at 3:00 a.m.

This is how you learn who people really are—and how they decide who you are.

I remembered names I heard mentioned in meetings and made a point to say, *I heard about you—great job.*

Because credibility wasn't assumed; it was earned—shift by shift, conversation by conversation.

Respect doesn't come from a title. It comes from paying attention.

I also learned how quickly people make assumptions. I was once called a five-letter word and told I didn't know a thing about anything—based on how I looked, and what someone assumed my life must have been like.

You have no idea how hard I had to work to be standing here.

They didn't know that I lost my dad at twenty-one, that I didn't have money for college, or that no one handed me anything.

And I wasn't about to explain myself just to make them more comfortable.

And I know this too: some people have had it better than me. Some have had it far worse. That's not the point.

Comparison doesn't build leadership—curiosity does.

The point is that **every person brings a story with them to work**. When we acknowledge that—and choose to support one another rather than judge the journey—we build trust.

And trust is where *real* leadership begins.

I thought about starting my own business after my life felt like it had gone belly-up—divorce, COVID, and a burnout that quietly started years earlier and never really stopped.

I can't keep doing it this way.

I thought about losing my dad, and how for nearly two decades I lived on adrenaline, moving from one responsibility to the next, saying yes to every training, every opportunity, every stretch assignment I could find. I was hungry—not just for success, but for understanding. Learning felt like being in control in a world that often wasn't.

Knowledge was the one thing that felt steady when everything else wasn't.

And woven through all of it was something my dad always said: *The one thing no one can ever take from you is your knowledge.*

He was right—and I carried that with me long before I knew how much I'd need it.

Looking back, I realize I didn't always have a single place to go for answers. I built my own library through experience, observation, mistakes, mentors, and moments of trial by fire.

This book exists because I know how isolating that journey can feel, and because I believe leaders deserve access to practical wisdom before they're forced to learn everything the hard way.

This book also exists because there wasn't one place where the real voices of people in business were brought together by HR professionals, specialists in wellbeing, finance, operations, and leadership, alongside the business owners themselves. The people doing the work rarely get to tell the story.

The people behind the decisions. The people shaping workplaces every day.

No two people are the same. No two journeys look alike. And yet, for decades, workplaces have tried to manage people as if they do—through one-size-fits-all rules, rigid processes, and employee handbooks that stretch well past a hundred pages. Somewhere along the way, we confused compliance with connection.

I've always said I'm not your typical HR person. Not because structure doesn't matter—but because paperwork alone doesn't build trust, loyalty, or strong cultures. People do. *People always have.*

What has always motivated me is making workplaces better—creating environments where leaders are the kind of people others actually want to work for and with.

I believe deeply in bringing people together. I don't believe I know best. Instead, I believe in weaving people's stories, experiences, and perspectives together—because that's how I've grown, how I've become better, and how real progress happens. **No one builds something meaningful *alone.***

Inside these pages, you'll find real stories paired with practical tools. Each chapter reflects lived experience and offers approaches you can actually use—because insight without action doesn't change anything.

As you read, you'll notice the diversity of voices represented here. While each contributor brings their own story and expertise, a shared truth runs through every chapter: **Strong businesses are built through people, not in spite of them.**

When leaders invest in people intentionally, they build more than profitable businesses. They build trust. Loyalty. Cultures people want to be part of. ***And legacies worth leaving behind.***

If you've ever known—deep down—that success depends on more than what's written in a business plan, ***this book was written for you.***

PART I

WHY IS THIS SO HARD?

THE HUMAN SIDE OF GROWTH

CHAPTER 1

THE BUSINESS OF BRINGING PEOPLE TOGETHER

WHAT YOU LEARN WHEN YOU'RE NOT THE OBVIOUS CHOICE

Susan S. Mahaffee, SPHR, SHRM-SCP, NDCCDP, CEC

*"You may encounter many defeats, but you must not be defeated.
In fact, it may be necessary to encounter the defeats,
so you can know who you are, what you can rise from,
how you can still come out of it."*

- Maya Angelou

MY STORY

We learn early what it feels like to be chosen.

Or not.

I still remember days in elementary school where I'd be standing in line for kickball, hoping my name would be called before the end, watching the captains scan the group, knowing exactly where the favorites stood—and where the rest of us landed.

Business can feel a lot like that. Especially when it turns into a quiet popularity contest—who gets the meeting, who gets the contract, who gets picked.

But here's what I've learned after years in business and leadership: **It's not sales or strategy that make a business successful. It's people.**

And if you've ever walked into a business and immediately felt turned off, you already know this is true. Maybe someone was complaining behind the counter. Maybe they looked annoyed when you were there. Maybe you overheard a conversation that made it clear no one felt valued or supported.

You didn't need a mission statement to tell you something was off—you felt it.

CUSTOMERS DON'T SEPARATE THE COMPANY FROM THE PERSON STANDING IN FRONT OF THEM.

Tone, posture, side comments, eye rolls—those moments *are* the brand. Culture doesn't live in a handbook. It lives in the hallway conversation that a customer overhears.

That's also why customer-facing roles matter so much. Your people are either selling trust for you—or quietly eroding it.

SCARCITY, POPULARITY, AND THE "PICK ME" FEELING

When I first started my business, holding onto that belief wasn't always easy.

There were moments when it felt like the same old lineup. Like being lined up and hoping someone would pick you—not last, not out of obligation, but because they actually wanted you there.

I hated that feeling as a kid. And there it was again—in my business.

I wasn't built for popularity contests. I was often the tallest girl—braces, glasses, a "funny" Central European last name people stumbled over. I didn't scream prom queen, and I didn't suddenly become the obvious choice just because I started a company.

Early on, it was easy to feel scarcity, to believe every opportunity mattered too much, that if someone chose another consultant, another firm, another voice, it meant something about my worth.

But over time, I learned something that changed how I show up. There is work for everyone. And not everyone is for you.

That shift—from scarcity to abundance—wasn't hollow, it was freeing. And it allowed me to lead, advise, and serve from a place of calm instead of hunger.

"THOSE PEOPLE ARE MY SPECIALTY"

There's a line I've said for years.

When someone warns me, "Just so you know, they're difficult," I usually smile and say, "Those people are my specialty."

What I've learned is that "difficult" is rarely about temperament. It's usually about not feeling heard, not feeling safe, or not trusting that someone is telling you the truth.

My approach has always been simple: patience, listening, helping people feel seen—and not walking into the room with an agenda.

I've worked with literal millionaires—and even a billionaire—for years. Titles and money never intimidated me. What mattered was having the courage to say the things that needed to be said.

And courage doesn't come from confidence alone. It comes from principles.

I was raised on them. And when things get tough—when the answers aren't clear, when emotions are high, when power dynamics are real—principles are what you lean on.

A CAREER-DEFINING MOMENT OF CLARITY

There was a moment—much later in my career—that shaped me in a profound way.

Someone with significant power over my future referred to me as "very female." Not quietly. Not subtly. And not as a compliment.

What made the moment even more disorienting was this: at the same time, this person wanted me on their team. They were actively offering me a role while talking down to me. It was a contradiction that stopped me in my tracks—being diminished and recruited—all at the same time.

When I shared this with my husband at the time, he said something that mattered deeply to me. (We're no longer married, but that doesn't change what he helped me realize about myself that day.)

He said, "If you don't stand up to that, you're not the person I thought you were."

And even now, I carry that with me.

What stayed with me wasn't just the comment itself. It was the realization that this wasn't about me at all.

When someone disrespects you while simultaneously wanting your talent, judgment, and leadership—that tells you everything you need to know about *them*.

But recognizing that takes emotional intelligence. And it takes professional maturity.

I didn't have that clarity early in my career. It took experience, mistakes, and hard-earned perspective to understand that power dynamics often reveal more about the person wielding them than the person on the receiving end. That moment didn't harden me. It sharpened me.

I learned that strong leaders don't absorb disrespect to stay safe. They respond from alignment. And they trust themselves enough to see the situation clearly.

FIRM IN BUSINESS, SOFT AT HEART

I've often said that I might be firm—and that's true. But it's important to say where that firmness lives.

That's me in business. Not in my parenting. Not in my personal life.

Outside of work, I've often been the one who gives more than I should, patient to a fault, willing to absorb more than my share.

But in my work, I learned something early: people don't benefit from leaders who disappear when things get uncomfortable. They benefit from leaders who can stay steady, grounded, and honest—especially when the answers aren't easy.

I've always prided myself on resilience. It's the one thing I know how to do.

Rise up.

Get better.

Be stronger than before.

There's a country song that says it best—*I've got a heart like a truck.* Banged up. Scratched along the way. But still running. Still showing up. Still willing to carry the load.

That resilience didn't come out of nowhere.

When I was younger, there were always kids who seemed more popular. They had the cool shoes, the right jeans, the things everyone thought mattered. And I remember saying to myself, *That's fine. I know I'll go farther than this when we grow up.* Not out of spite. Out of survival.

I learned to swallow rejection, to get better at hearing no, and to build strong self-talk that said: *Keep going. Improve. Stay focused.*

Most of us have been there.

And I don't say this to judge anyone. I'm simply naming a truth: When you don't fit the mold, you either shrink—or you build resilience. I chose the second.

That's what shows up in my work. That's what allows me to sit with difficult people, to say hard things with care, and to create spaces where others feel safe enough to be challenged.

SAFE ENOUGH TO BE CHALLENGED

Growth doesn't happen because someone is nice; it happens because someone is honest *in a way you can receive.*

I've always tried to create spaces—whether with clients, teams, or leaders—where people feel safe enough to be challenged. Where they know I'm not there to win, perform, or protect my ego. I'm there to help them be better.

Years later, when former employees reach out or comment, "You were the best HR person I ever had," I feel it—and I know it came from leading with integrity, courage, and humanity.

Coach Mike Krzyzewski once said he was a leader who just happened to coach basketball. I'm a leader who just so happens to specialize in HR.

TOUCHING THE WHITE FENCE

There's a moment in life where you know you've made it.

Not because of money.

Not because of titles.

But because of impact.

For me, it's like touching the white fence. It's the quiet knowing that your life has purpose, that people were better because they crossed your path, and that you helped someone stand taller, think more clearly, or lead more honestly.

People don't just buy what you sell; they buy how you make them feel—and whether they trust that feeling to last.

Because in the end, it's never just about the plan. It's never just about the product. People buy people. And when you lead with courage, curiosity, and principles, they don't just buy once. They remember **you**.

THE TOOL

THE "NOT THE OBVIOUS CHOICE" MIRROR

When situations get tense, emotional, or personal, I come back to this "mirror". It's my way of holding up the questions and thoughts that I'd want reflected back to me when I'm going to make a decision, when the answer isn't straightforward or easy.

As I often tell leaders, ***be hard on the issue, not the people.***

That mindset keeps the focus where it belongs—on solving the problem—without attacking, blaming, or damaging the relationships we still need to lead, work, and move forward together.

Use these four questions to help you think through something emotionally charged, confusing, or when you just need to sense-check yourself.

This isn't about being "soft." It's about being **clear, fair, and *human*.**

1. Where might this person feel "almost picked"?

Before responding, I pause and ask where this person may feel overlooked, dismissed, or uncertain about their standing.

You might hear yourself say:

- "I want to understand what this situation has been like for you."
- "Before we talk about next steps, help me see this from your side."
- "Something about this feels bigger than the surface issue—am I right?"

This doesn't excuse behavior. It helps you understand what's *underneath it.*

2. What is the real issue—stripped of personality?

This is where clarity replaces frustration. Instead of reacting to tone or emotion, I focus on what actually needs to change.

You might say:

- "Let's separate how this feels from what needs to happen."
- "Here's the standard we need to meet, regardless of how we got here."
- "This isn't about you as a person—it's about this expectation."

This keeps conversations clean and fair—especially when emotions are high.

3. Am I trying to win—or trying to be fair?

This is often the quiet turning point. I ask myself whether my reaction is about protecting my authority—or protecting the work, the relationship, and the principle.

You might internally check:

- "Would I say this the same way if power were equal?"
- "Am I responding, or reacting?"
- "Is my goal to be right—or to be effective?"

When leaders get this wrong, trust erodes quickly. When they get it right, it multiplies.

4. What response helps this person rise—not retreat?

This is where firmness and care meet.

You don't avoid the hard truth—you deliver it in a way that preserves dignity.

You might say:

- "I need to be direct here, because I believe in your ability to handle it."
- "This is a hard conversation, but it's an important one."
- "I'm holding this line because it matters—not because I don't value you."

The goal isn't compliance. The goal is growth.

WHY THIS LENS WORKS

When you're not the obvious choice, you learn how to choose people well.

You learn how to:

- listen without collapsing
- be firm without being cruel
- name issues without attacking identity
- create safety *and* momentum

That's where real leadership lives. And over time, those small, steady moments add up—in trust, loyalty, and results.

Great leadership isn't built in grand gestures. It's built in a series of small moments, handled well. Those moments become your leadership signature—and people are always watching how you handle them.

Susan S. Mahaffee is the President and Founder of People Rise LLC, a certified woman-owned HR consulting and leadership advisory firm that partners with small to mid-size businesses, entrepreneurs, and family-owned organizations. With more than two decades of experience in HR leadership, executive coaching, and organizational strategy, Susan helps leaders navigate the people moments that shape culture, trust, and long-term success.

Susan is a proud graduate of Johnson & Wales University, long known as *America's Career University* for its emphasis on learning that extends beyond the classroom—preparing students for real work, real decisions, and real responsibility. That focus deepened her love for the workplace and gave her the confidence to take the leap at a time when affording college was hard, but the investment felt purposeful.

Susan often credits her leadership philosophy to lessons learned early in life—especially from her father, affectionately known as "Chef Bank," whose kitchen became her first classroom for leadership, accountability, and care. Those lessons continue to shape her work today and the legacy she is building for her son.

In addition to her consulting work, Susan is a Certified Executive Leadership Coach, speaker, and host of *The Employee Help Desk* podcast. She is also a member of the Leadership Anne Arundel (LAA) Flagship Class of 2026 and serves as Vice Chair of Governance for the Alliance for the Chesapeake Bay.

She is a contributing author in *We Lead, Volume 3*, where she wrote Chapter 20, **Building an Authentic, People-Centered Business—Own Your Style, Voice, and Impact**. Susan was proud to be part of the book's achievement of Amazon Bestseller status in six categories. That experience reinforced for her what's possible when trusted voices come together around shared values and purpose.

Susan believes people choose to work with her because they align with her approach to doing business—clear, principled, and relationship-driven. She lives in Severna Park, Maryland, with her son, Peter, and their lovable Shih Tzu, Rocket, who—true to form—never misses a chance to make her feel chosen.

Connect with Susan:

Website: www.peoplerisellc.com

LinkedIn: https://www.linkedin.com/in/smahaffee/

Instagram: @peoplerisellc

Book Community Instagram: @whenpeoplerise

Podcast: The Employee Help Desk is available on both Apple and Spotify, as well as https://www.peoplerisellc.com/podcast

Media & Speaking Inquiries: info@peoplerisellc.com

CHAPTER 2

WELLNESS IS NOT A PERK

WHEN PEOPLE THRIVE, BUSINESSES OUTPERFORM

Elizabeth Harris, MS, RDN, Wellbeing Strategist

MY STORY

Like many things in life, I didn't go looking for workplace wellness. It found me.

For years, I've worked as a dietitian in private practice, supporting high-achieving people to improve their nutrition, health, and wellbeing without getting trapped in the failed dieting cycle. After working with hundreds of individuals, I saw the same patterns surfacing again and again.

Most people aren't lacking in nutrition knowledge or even motivation. They generally know which foods are more or less nutritious and which healthy habits are recommended. Nearly everyone I work with *wants* to take better care of themselves and their bodies.

"Elizabeth," they tell me, "I know what I *should* be doing. I'm a very capable person in every other area of my life. But food is the one nut I just can't crack. I can't seem to make anything stick."

I usually respond with a question. "What trips you up the most?" The answers are almost always the same. Time, stress, exhaustion, and the pressure to do everything perfectly.

In other words, it's typically not *what* to do that trips them up. It's *how*.

What they're really asking me is, "How do I make room for healthy habits when I have so many competing priorities?" "How do I find the time or the energy to shop for and prepare nourishing foods, exercise, rest, sleep, hydrate, manage stress, or support my mental health while juggling work, parenting, paying bills, caring for aging parents, and everything else that comes my way?"

Over and over, I hear the same things. People feel overwhelmed and exhausted even just thinking about it.

I ask all new clients the following question: "Where does self-care fall on your to-do list?" They often answer, "It's been so long since I've tried, I don't even know what self-care is anymore." Or they look at me like a deer in headlights and say, "It's at the bottom." Or simply, "nowhere."

And honestly, I understand where they're coming from. For a time after opening my private practice, I struggled to prioritize my own self-care. Suddenly, I was sitting most of the day, working through lunch, missing workouts, and cooking fewer meals at home—all while teaching others how to care for their health! My family started commenting, "Are we eating leftovers or takeout *again*?" Unhappily, I found that my average daily step count plummeted (as in, it fell off a cliff!). *I don't feel good,* I realized. *I didn't start my business to help others improve their health while undermining my own.*

Fortunately, I was able to use this moment as a turning point to reprioritize my healthy habits. I understand what my clients are up against on a personal level. Even with all my training, resources, and flexibility as a dietitian and an entrepreneur, my wellness took a back seat for longer than it should have. *If that can happen to me, imagine how impossible it must feel for people navigating far less supportive environments and circumstances.*

Unfortunately, the patterns I saw in private practice were impossible to ignore, and they pointed to something much bigger.

TWO CULTURAL FORCES THAT MAKE HEALTHY LIVING FEEL HARDER THAN IT SHOULD

First, we live in a toxic diet culture that deeply impacts how people think about food, health, and their bodies. These beliefs don't stop at the office door. They show up in how people fuel themselves during the workday, how they talk about food and exercise with colleagues, how they're perceived at work, and how confidently they show up in their professional roles.

Diet culture isn't just about weight loss, and you don't have to be "on a diet" to be profoundly impacted by it. It's a deep-rooted, societal belief system that promotes a rigid and narrow view of health. Diet culture equates thinness with health, assumes that larger bodies are less healthy, and frames an ideal body size as something you earn through discipline and good behavior. It ignores critical factors like genetics, environment, access, and other social determinants of health.

Instead, health is treated as both a personal responsibility and a measure of character and worth. If you're disciplined with food or exercise, you're seen as virtuous and healthy. If you're not, you "failed" or don't have enough willpower. Diet culture encourages quick fixes, rigid and restrictive rules about eating, and a good-versus-bad mindset towards food and exercise.

In workplace settings, these beliefs result in many people being chronically under-nourished, ignoring basic body cues like hunger or fatigue, or being mentally preoccupied with food or weight concerns. Many internalize the belief that their bodies are being judged before their body of work, eroding confidence and making it harder for them to contribute at their highest level. Over time, this doesn't just impact individual health; it means organizations are missing out on their employees' fullest potential.

Once you see the harms of diet culture, you cannot unsee them. It fuels all-or-nothing thinking, cycles of restriction and overeating, guilt, shame, body image struggles, and increased risk for disordered eating. Over time, these patterns can diminish motivation and confidence, making it feel impossible for many people to consistently care for their nutrition or health.

Diet culture is a harmful barrier to genuine, whole health. And yet, the more people I worked with, the clearer it became that it's not the only cultural force working against us. Many of my clients don't just grapple with harmful food and body beliefs. They also struggle to build healthy habits while navigating demanding jobs that leave them with little time, energy, or capacity for self-care.

Many workplaces say they value employee wellbeing, and some genuinely do. Sadly, others don't. Too many people are overworked and under-appreciated, expected to remain reachable around the clock. Clients regularly share that their schedules are so packed and their responsibilities so constant that they barely have time to eat or even use the bathroom, let alone rest, recharge, or engage in any meaningful health-promoting behaviors!

When employees experience chronic stress and burnout, healthy habits stop feeling helpful and start seeming like one more obligation on an already overwhelming to-do list.

In short, diet culture demands constant discipline and self-monitoring, while many workplaces leave people with little bandwidth, flexibility, or practical support to prioritize their health. No wonder so many people feel so lost or discouraged!

TURNING INSIGHT INTO ACTION

At a certain point, I realized I could help people transform their relationship with food and build healthier habits. But if they were stuck in workplaces that didn't support their wellbeing, they would still struggle.

Quite simply, without cultural support, even the best nutrition or health guidance will always fall short.

This realization pushed me to look at wellbeing through a wider lens. I saw how much culture and environment matter, and why my work needed to expand beyond one-to-one nutrition counseling. *I can have a much bigger impact and support far more people by expanding into employee wellbeing. By helping to shape healthier workplace cultures, I can better support individual health behaviors, too.*

At its core, my work is grounded in a simple belief: health is our first and most fundamental source of wealth. When we don't have our health, everything else suffers or gets sidelined, including our job responsibilities.

This belief is reinforced every time I work in various organizations. When people are encouraged and feel supported to care for themselves, the impact is far-reaching. Energy improves. Focus sharpens. Creativity, engagement, problem-solving, and retention all rise. Healthy people build healthy, thriving businesses.

Contrary to popular belief, wellness isn't a perk. It's essential. As with operations, technology, marketing, or product and service development, investing in employee wellbeing is a critical infrastructure that determines a company's performance, results, and lasting success.

That said, as I dug into workplace wellbeing, I noticed an obvious gap in the way many companies approach wellness, if they offer it at all. They may offer workshops, gym memberships, health screenings, and other programs aimed at changing individual behaviors, but they miss acknowledging or addressing the workplace environment that shapes them. Or they may have a wellness-oriented culture but fail to challenge the harmful diet culture messages that detract from health and wellbeing and harm people's relationships with food, movement, and their bodies.

My work lives at the intersection of these two cultural forces. I work to dismantle toxic diet culture and promote weight-inclusive workplaces where people feel safe, supported, and respected, while also helping organizations create cultures that promote and prioritize employees' physical, mental, and emotional wellbeing, or what I like to call their "whole health."

This work goes far beyond any single discipline. Nutrition is critical, of course, but it's only one piece of a much larger whole health puzzle. That's why I ultimately partnered with a values-aligned mental health professional and a personal trainer to deliver holistic wellness programs to a wide range of organizations. Together, we've built an extensive network of wellness experts, including breathwork healers, massage therapists, yoga instructors, and a host of others, so we can support wellbeing at the organizational level with an integrated, multidisciplinary approach.

YOU WON'T BELIEVE THESE RIPPLE EFFECTS

Let me share a powerful example of what's possible when employee wellbeing is treated as a shared priority between management and employees from a preschool where I worked with the administration to craft a customized, year-long wellness program while also addressing diet culture head-on.

Early childhood education is a demanding profession, both physically and emotionally. Many of us entrust these educators with our children during formative years. We want the people caring for our kids to feel supported, energized, and able to show up at their best! Yet stress levels are often high and compensation rates low, making burnout, absenteeism, and turnover persistent challenges across the field.

Teachers typically have tight schedules, coordinated bathroom breaks, inflexible lunch periods, and limited opportunities to grab a snack or take a quick breather during the school day. Plus, they juggle behavior challenges, rapid transitions, parent concerns, and kids' fluctuating emotions.

So, I was particularly excited when the administration of these preschools reached out for support in bringing employee wellbeing resources to their teachers and staff. After discussing their goals and identifying some of the most pressing challenges facing their teams, which included frequent teacher absences, limited time and tools to support nourishment during the workday, and growing concerns about the messages being modeled around food and health, I designed a wellness program centered around three core objectives:

1. **Equip teachers and staff with practical, accessible wellness tools and guidance they could realistically use during the school day and integrate into life outside of work.**

2. **Support food and body confidence for both employees and children by raising awareness about diet culture and the impact that common language, policies, and practices can have on body image, individual behaviors, and lifelong beliefs about food, health, and ourselves.**

3. **Embed wellbeing into the school culture by making it a consistent priority throughout the school year (and beyond).**

By incorporating most of our workshops into their existing professional development initiatives, the program was thoughtfully designed to meet teachers where they were, both in terms of time and capacity.

We kicked off the program with a workshop titled *How to Grow Kids with Food and Body Confidence.* I began by sharing why this topic matters so deeply, highlighting research that shows body dissatisfaction and dieting behaviors begin far earlier than many adults realize, *even in early elementary years!* This helped get teachers' immediate attention and buy-in and opened meaningful conversations about diet culture, its impact, and the importance of how we talk about and approach food, movement, and bodies. Teachers recognized how their own beliefs and behaviors influence kids' developing relationships with food and their bodies, as well as their own personal wellbeing and healthy habits.

With this foundation in place and a shared understanding of the harmful role that diet culture plays in workplaces, classrooms, and personal health, we turned our focus to equipping teachers with tools and skills to improve their nutrition, manage chronic stress, and build lasting healthy habits.

Throughout the year, the program focused on practical, realistic ways teachers could support their wellbeing within the demands of their workdays. Topics included nourishing for a full school day, tools to complete the stress cycle in just a few minutes, meal prep strategies for busy professionals, healthy habit building, simple mindfulness practices to support nervous system regulation, and more.

We delivered these through a mix of hands-on workshops, engaging team-building challenges, multimedia resources, and ongoing access to me for questions, support, and sharing wins. What made this program so successful is that leadership intentionally modeled what it looks like to prioritize one's wellbeing. They clearly communicated their core belief that employees are valued not just as *workers* but as *whole people* whose health and wellbeing matter.

The results were powerful and more far-reaching than even I could have predicted. Teachers quickly recognized the importance of addressing and eliminating diet culture from the preschool environment, and they supported one another in doing so. They shifted how they talk with children about food and exercise. For example, they no longer tell kids they "have to eat their healthy foods first," and they stopped referring to "junk foods." They upgraded the snack options in their classrooms, reached out to chat about their own health needs, and began sharing what they were learning about growing kids with food and body confidence in conversations with families.

School leadership reported a noticeable and positive shift in tone across both preschools. "The culture is more focused on nourishment and wellbeing, less about sharing how run down everyone feels," they reported. Over the course of the year, they observed greater excitement and engagement around healthy habits and meal prep, with teachers reinforcing one another's efforts and creating a shared sense of momentum. The impact of prioritizing wellbeing extended beyond individual employees, positively shaping and benefiting the entire school community, including children, families, teachers, staff, and leadership alike.

Plus, absenteeism remains lower years later.

I love this example and want to emphasize that this work isn't limited to schools. Across the wide variety of organizations I partner with, when people are valued as whole humans and cultures are thoughtfully curated to support and prioritize physical, mental, and emotional wellbeing, everyone benefits. Employees thrive. Leadership is strengthened. And businesses are better positioned to outperform.

THE TOOL

The following **Culture Check** isn't a test or a scorecard. It's a tool to reflect on whether the daily realities of your workplace make it easier or harder for people to care for themselves. While every organization is unique, there are some shared considerations that can reveal how well wellbeing is supported.

As you read through the statements below, notice your first reaction.

WORKPLACE WELLNESS CULTURE CHECK

In my workplace…

1. **People can eat during the workday without rushing, feeling guilty for taking the time to eat, or working through lunch as the norm.**

2. **When meals and snacks are provided, they are nutrient-dense and help me feel well-fueled to do my job.**

3. **Food choices, exercise, and bodies are not moralized, commented on, or used as a measure of discipline or worth.**

4. **Movement throughout the workday is supported or encouraged with things like walking meetings, an on-site gym, regular stretch breaks, optional standing desks, drop-in movement sessions, calendar buffers between meetings, wellness stipends, etc.**

5. Taking short, well-timed breaks is accepted and respected, not quietly discouraged or reprimanded.

6. Workloads are realistic, and people are trusted to meet expectations in ways that allow for flexibility and balance.

7. Employees are not praised for working around the clock, exhaustion, or "pushing through" at the expense of their physical or mental health.

8. Employees feel psychologically safe asking for what they need to do their jobs well.

9. People are encouraged to take non-working vacations and supported instead of judged when they need to call in sick or take a mental health day.

10. Employees are not expected to be reachable or "on" at all hours of the day and night, and leadership respects these boundaries.

11. Mental health needs or conditions are not stigmatized, shamed, or gossiped about.

12. Opportunities for social engagement and bonding are provided and encouraged.

13. Leadership models and encourages engaging in activities that promote physical, mental, and emotional health.

14. People are treated and respected as whole humans, not just as workers or for their productivity.

NOW PAUSE AND REFLECT:

How many of these statements feel true?

How many feel attainable but not yet in place?

How many feel out of reach or noticeably absent?

If you answered no to many of these questions, it doesn't mean your workplace doesn't care about wellbeing. But the culture may have unintentionally evolved in ways that overlooked wellbeing as an important component of productivity and profits. Or leadership may not currently have the language, tools, or roadmap to better support employee wellness.

If this is the case, please know you're not alone, and workplace culture *can* be positively changed. One way to do this is to partner with a wellbeing strategist or team who can assess your current culture, identify gaps, and provide thoughtful consulting, strategy, and boots-on-the-ground services to build a healthier, more sustainable, and ultimately more successful workplace.

HERE ARE TWO WAYS YOU CAN GET STARTED:

Download my free resource, 10 Simple Ways to Improve Your Workplace Wellness Culture Immediately

It's full of simple strategies you can implement right away to support employee wellbeing with resources people will value and use. You can access it at www.elizabethharrisnutrition.com/workplace-culture

Schedule a Workspace Review

My team and I will take a thoughtful look at your current work environment and culture, identify where wellbeing is and isn't being supported, and provide clear, actionable, fully customized recommendations to better support the health and long-term vitality of your employees and your business.

Email me at livehealthy@elizabethharrisnutrition.com to get started.

Elizabeth Harris is a registered dietitian, certified Intuitive Eating counselor, speaker, entrepreneur, and media spokesperson. She is the co-host of *Wellness Rebranded*, a top 2% globally ranked podcast that focuses on food, fitness, and feelings for women in midlife.

Elizabeth specializes in creating weight-inclusive, evidence-based wellness programs that support both individuals and organizations. Through customized employee wellbeing initiatives, workshops, retreats, and leadership programming, she partners with companies nationwide to reduce burnout, promote healthy habits, and create workplace cultures where people can thrive, physically, mentally, and emotionally.

At the core of Elizabeth's work is an *add-in* approach to nutrition rooted in the principles of Intuitive Eating. She believes food is meant to be enjoyed, movement should make you happy, and we've all got better things to do than count carbs or calories! In her private practice, Elizabeth helps individuals break free from chronic dieting, make peace with food and their bodies, and build a lasting, sustainable approach to nourishment that goes far beyond any meal plan.

Elizabeth holds a master's degree in Nutrition, Healthspan, and Longevity from the University of Southern California and a bachelor's degree in Russian language and Slavic and Eastern European Studies from the University of Connecticut. Outside of her work, you'll find her keeping backyard bees, gardening, reading voraciously, and traveling the world with her husband and three adult kids—hitting every available farmers' market along the way.

Connect with Elizabeth:

Instagram: https://www.instagram.com/elizabethharrisnutrition/

Facebook: https://www.facebook.com/elizabethharrisnutrition/
http://www.facebook.com/groups/healthandhealingwithintuitiveeating/

Website: http://www.elizabethharrisnutrition.com/

Book a complimentary whole health strategy session:
https://elizabethharrisnutrition.com/booking

CHAPTER 3

ADDRESSING CHILDHOOD TRAUMA IN THE WORKPLACE

INCREASE HEALING, PRODUCTIVITY, AND YOUR BOTTOM LINE

Dr. Pamela J. Pine

MY STORY

Mitchell is a creative spirit, who, after trying various types of work to sustain himself—in real estate, home health care, and creative arts programs—ended up in his 40s having slept with over 400 people, depressed and despondent, regularly using substances to self-medicate and cope, unable to focus on work, and, ultimately, supported by family due to an inability to hold down a job. While walking with him one day, head down, he told me, "Everyone leaves me."

Of the 10 recognized adverse childhood experiences[1] (ACEs), Mitchell has six of them. If someone has one, it will likely affect one's life, and if one has one, one often has more. If one has six, the psychological, neurological, behavioral, physical, and/or social/economic problems are often overwhelming.

The physical outcomes due to chronic stress (long-term physiological dysfunction, inflammation, and immune system weakening that ultimately correlate with increased risks of heart disease, cancer, diabetes, obesity, stroke, chronic obstructive pulmonary disease/COPD, liver disease, and chronic pain) and mental health issues (e.g., depression, anxiety, bipolar disorder, PTSD, aggressiveness, sociopathy, and more) *result in increased absenteeism and lower workplace performance.*

> "In 2010 dollars, the estimated average **lifetime cost per victim [emphasis mine]** of nonfatal child maltreatment was estimated at $144,360 in productivity losses [alone, not including child or adult health care costs, criminal justice costs, etc.!]… costs associated with child maltreatment place a distinct and substantial burden on the U.S. economy, underscoring the importance of child abuse prevention and intervention efforts to reduce the prevalence of maltreatment across the United States…"
>
> - One Place (2023). Report: The Economic Impact of Child Abuse. One Place, Onslow, NC.

The impact on health, wellness, social systems, diminished labor productivity, high turnover, and reduced consumer demand totals hundreds of billions in losses annually in the U.S. alone.[2]

---

1 The 10 Adverse Childhood Experiences (ACEs) are as follows: 1. Physical Abuse, 2. Sexual Abuse, 3. Emotional Abuse, 4. Physical Neglect, 5. Emotional Neglect, 6. Mental Illness, 7. Incarcerated Relative, 8. Mother Treated Violently, 9. Substance Use, 10. Divorce

2 "In the United States alone, the total lifetime cost associated with just one year of confirmed cases of child maltreatment is estimated at $428 billion (The Economic Burden of Child Maltreatment in the United States and Implications for Prevention, Centers for Disease Control and Prevention)." In One Place (2023).

Why is this important to *you*? What if workplace managers and human resource leaders knew what to look for as red flags and how to help? Signs of regular sickness, depression, professional presentation, lower job performance…

Businesses of all kinds—corporate entities and non-profits alike—have a role to play. There are steps *you* can take to address this in your place of work, no matter what you do or how big or small your workplace is. With the number of people affected, you're sure to impact not only people's lives and communities, but also the health and well-being of your business.

I have now spent the last 25 years doing what I do—trying to increase awareness, understanding, and action on childhood trauma and protection. I do get frustrated at times. *How do I make this all stick?*

Of late, I've turned my full attention to the adults, to their workplaces and, relatedly, to their leadership, staff, families, and their well-being, psychologically, physically, spiritually, and economically. In other words, to *you*. *You* can make a difference in your workplace.

*　*　*

Working in the child trauma and protection field for a quarter of a century, I've heard hundreds of stories.

Paula, ultimately, after a very chaotic adolescence and young adulthood abusing drugs and alcohol, built herself up to a substantial position in education, only to wind up unable to sustain it, given severe physical and mental health issues that began in her 30s. Our paths crossed when she was in her 50s.

"Pam, I'm living in a moldy attic," she said. "My rent is still too high for this place, and I feel sick all the time. I'm writing a book about my life," she went on. "I think it's going to be great. I think it will make me lots of money. Then I can move out of this place."

I knew Kelly from her professional, successful, and lucrative work in health-drink product sales in corporate America. She texted me one day, while in her 40s: "Is this really you?" "Why are you pretending to be Pamela Pine?"

"It's me," I assured her.

"Okay. Pam, can you give me some money to help me?"

She continued to unravel psychologically and financially after no longer being able to keep her secret under wraps or cope with trying to address it.

For Marjorie, a professionally successful survivor and psychologist, there are no more Thanksgivings or other holidays for her or her daughter with family.

"You're lying," said one sister after Marjorie went public about her pillar-of-the-community perpetrator father. The other just slammed the phone down when Marjorie called. Depression followed, which had repercussions for her personal and professional life.

* * *

By the point in my profession that I began to learn about all this, I obtained both significant educational and career levels, having worked around the world with agencies like the World Health Organization (WHO), the United States Agency for International Development (USAID), the United Nations Population Fund (UNFPA), the World Bank, and others, on some of the world's most critical health issues. I stepped into worlds that looked, sounded, and behaved differently in Yemen, Ethiopia, Egypt, Zambia, and many other countries. I hold a PhD in Health Education, a Master of Public Health (MPH), and a Master of International Affairs (MAIA), and completed undergraduate coursework in medicine (which I did not finish) at prestigious universities. I knew a fair amount about the world and its problems.

But I hadn't had one course nor focus on childhood trauma!

In 2000, while sitting in an international health company office in Washington, D.C., I opened an email with information from the Centers for Disease Control and Prevention (CDC). It presented information on interpersonal violence (IPV). Given that my sister was a therapist in California who obtained a substantial positive reputation in helping survivors of child sexual abuse (CSA) heal, I began reading there.

All the information I read on the CDC website was brand new to me. What I found out was more than alarming! Child sexual abuse, affecting currently about one in four to six girls and one in six to eight boys in the U.S. alone (which translates into more than 55 million adult survivors in the U.S., with similar types of percentages seen worldwide), wreaks havoc.

The children are usually abused by someone they know (e.g., fathers, mothers, brothers, uncles, aunts, cousins, coaches, teachers, neighbors)—people who should be protecting them but are substantially hurting them, crossing all acceptable or tolerable boundaries.

The damage is physical, psychological, and neurological and has major implications for their childhood, adolescent, and adult selves and wellbeing. This trauma affects long-term relationships and the onset of health problems, including, as I noted above, chronic disease and early death. Most survivors don't say anything—if they ever say anything—until their early 50s, so they don't get help for decades.

There are also severe ramifications for their families (often critically affecting the current and next generations), communities, school and work environments, and societies—in terms of functioning and economic outcomes. Add on the impact of other ACEs, and we are living in a catastrophe that has ramifications for us all.

I walked down my company's long corridors, which housed many offices branching off them, and asked my esteemed colleagues, one by one: "Have you had any education in childhood trauma?" "No" was the only answer I received.

Why, I asked myself and colleagues, were we, individually, as communities, as societies, not addressing these issues: child sexual abuse, child physical abuse, child neglect, violence, and dysfunctional drug and alcohol use in households, and the other ACEs?

I set about doing something about this, designing and conducting research into why people don't want to address these issues, and applying that research. "How does one raise awareness about an issue that no one wants to talk about?" was the focus. I started with massive advocacy events that involved thousands and got major media attention, and educational and training programs designed to bring awareness, understanding, and action to a wide swath of individuals, including parents, educators, therapists, clinicians, first responders, and the wider public.

I began an international non-profit organization, Stop the Silence®: Stop Child Sexual Abuse, Inc., under which to conduct crucial awareness, education, and training for broad audiences.

Nadine, a lawyer/colleague friend, warned me, "Pam, don't put CSA in the name of the organization. Everyone will avoid you."

I remained steadfast: "But, Nadine," I said with a sigh, "I very consciously chose the subtitle of the organization's name. When people put our ads out in the media, they'll have to say the name out loud! If we can't talk about it, if we can't even say it, we can't do anything about it!"

I was right. Our first ad about our upcoming major event on a major radio station made me smile. A prominent, female broadcaster, reading our ad—obviously for the first time—about the first (2004) Race to Stop the Silence®, an 8K/10K foot race around communities in Washington, D.C. (which I conducted every year for ten years in April during Child Abuse Awareness Month), stumbled over our name in those early days. "And this hour brought to you by. . .uh. . .by. . .uh [voice gets lower, slower, and strained] Stop the Silence-Stop Child Sexual Abuse, Inc." Later ads no longer had the stumbling.

The resulting programming was exhilarating to watch with prominent speakers, lots of publicity (TV, radio, newspapers, magazines, billboards), and waves and waves of people starting and finishing under a banner that stretched from one side of a D.C. boulevard to another and read "International Race to Stop the Silence® – Stop Child Sexual Abuse." Ultimately, at the Race's height, about 2,000 elite, regular, and support-of-the-issue runners (and walkers) and spectators in the streets of D.C. wore t-shirts that declared Stop the Silence®-Stop Child Sexual Abuse on their backs.

The race did what it was supposed to do—bring awareness, but my to-do lists came to span pages and pages, and, at times, *I* was seen racing around the office trying to get all that I knew needed to be done, done, feeling half-crazed myself sometimes with the weight, urgency, and sadness of it all.

* * *

Over the years, I've come up with answers as to why we don't want to and too often don't address these issues—anywhere. But we must—and companies are critical as a part of the effort.

When we put the words "child" and "sexual" in the same sentence, people squirm. We know that these words do not belong together. CSA, but other ACEs, as well, carry enormous fear, shame, blame, guilt, and stigma with them. These are never the child or adult survivors to hold, nor the non-offending others in their families, but they often do.

One day, I rode a train back home from the office. I was in the middle of planning that year's race and calling people and organizations for their support and involvement. I was in a public car with compartments that had seats facing each other, two forward and two backward, independent of the direction the train was going—four seats in a compartment with the mirror-image seating across the aisle.

"Hello, this is Dr. Pamela Pine, and I'm calling from Stop the Silence®: Stop Child Sexual Abuse, Inc., and we are planning...." "Hello, this is Dr. Pamela Pine, and I am calling from Stop the Silence®: Stop Child Sexual Abuse, Inc...." "Hello, this is Dr. Pamela Pine, and I'm calling from Stop the Silence®: Stop Child Sexual Abuse, Inc...."

After about the fifth call, the man directly across the aisle from me, facing in the same direction as me, looked sideways at me and harshly proclaimed: "Will you be quiet!?"

One very loud beat went by. The man facing me in the same compartment as mine turned toward the man admonishing me: "This is not a quiet car. She can say anything she wants to say. But *you* can leave."

I wondered for a moment if people would go fisticuffs over my telephone calls, but I realized the advocacy was getting somewhere. After assessing the situation for a moment, I continued. "Hello, this is Dr. Pamela Pine, and I am calling from Stop the Silence®: Stop Child Sexual Abuse, Inc...."

I spent a fair amount of effort and time at one point trying to get into the school systems to educate administrators, parents, teachers, and kids.

The kids are the easiest. I was invited in by individual teachers or principals.

"I'm going to read you a little story," I'd say to an auditorium of little kids.

It was a simple, non-explicit, picture, rhyming story penned by a colleague of mine about a little kid who didn't like the way s/he (the child was drawn in a non-definitive way, allowing the child to be a representation of a boy or a girl, with a neck-length bob and jeans) was being touched by someone and how the child's parents praised the child for letting them know. I read the rhyme in a sing-song kind of way. I read it again, then I asked the kids to fill in the final line of each stanza after I read the first three. And gleefully they complied.

Then, I said, "I brought some prizes with me. Raise your hand if you know what to do if someone is touching you in a way you don't like?"

Lots of hands went up. The "winners"—each one who was called on and answered the question being posed—came up and got their prizes.

But many school administrators have not been so inviting. One administrator initially began coordinating with me for a program for teachers but then went MIA. Not hearing from her, but having reserved the day on my calendar, I called her supervisor, merely trying to find out where and when.

The follow-up call I finally got from the original administrator went like this: "*Dr.* Pine, who the *hell* do you think you are? If and when we want your presence, we'll let you know." And she hung up.

Why? The adults working in education are often uncomfortable. Schools are often (usually, perhaps) not equipped to deal with the response of children coming forward. Do they have counseling support if faced with kids' needs? What are the parents going to say about this program?! And child abuse is a PR nightmare. *Sure,* I'd sarcastically think, my head jolting up, my eyes rolling up in my head, and my eyebrows shooting up with them, *let's worry more about what is said about the reaction to trying to prevent and mitigate than deal with preventing or addressing the issues themselves. Good plan.*

Oh, so many stories. Let's change them together! Organizations need to step up to create successful environments for their staff and their bottom lines—and for the sake of us all!

Remember that research I said I conducted when I began this journey? The one to find out how to raise awareness and ultimately change behavior about an issue that no one wants to talk about? It turns out that, more than media, more than anything else, what people respond to in terms of increasing their awareness, understanding, and changing their behavior related to this, thereby creating immediate personal, organizational, and generational change, are the people they know: family, friends, trusted associates (e.g., hairdressers), colleagues, clinicians, other service providers, and supervisors—*you*. Changing the current situation cannot be done without *you*.

THE TOOL

Companies can address Adverse Childhood Experiences (ACEs) with staff by fostering a trauma-informed, compassionate work culture that prioritizes psychological safety, mental health, and flexibility. Key actions include training managers to recognize signs of trauma, expanding Employee Assistance Programs (EAPs), encouraging open communication, and offering supportive, flexible policies.

KEY STRATEGIES FOR COMPANIES INCLUDE:

1. **Implementing Trauma-Informed Training: Educate leaders and HR staff on the science of ACEs and toxic stress, and their impact on performance, emphasizing understanding rather than judgment.**

2. **Enhancing EAPs and Benefits: Strengthen Employee Assistance Programs to offer accessible counseling, mental health resources, and support services.**

3. **Cultivating a Safe Environment: Create a culture where staff feel comfortable discussing mental health, using tools like "high fives" for recognition, and fostering compassion.**

4. **Adopting Flexible Policies: Offer flexible work hours, remote work options, and adequate paid time off to reduce employee stress.**

5. **Training in Supportive Communication: Train managers to hold private, supportive conversations focusing on root causes of underperformance rather than immediate disciplinary action.**

6. **Utilizing Community Resources: Connect employees with external resources for housing, food, or childcare, potentially using a "Community Resource Navigator" for confidential support.**

By focusing on these areas, organizations can reduce the impact of ACEs on productivity, improve employee well-being, and support overall resilience.

You can start like this: Learn more about the issues (about child maltreatment, but also about child maltreatment and its effect on the workplace). Check out information on our website (https://www.ivatcenters.org/stop-the-silence) or contact me for more information (pamelap@ivatcenters.org).

There are a few specific actions you can take to move this forward:

1. **Present the issues or bring in someone who knows them well to present them to leadership and staff.**

2. **Request consent and then conduct an anonymous, electronic poll (make sure to underscore to the staff that it is completely anonymous–remember, these are sensitive issues that often cause enormous pain, guilt, shame, and fear) to assess the staff members' ACE score and tell them why you're doing it.**

This will help you know how much of an issue ACEs pose in your company. You can include additional questions like:

- "How much do you think this affects your work?"

- "If the company could help you find a way to further address these issues, would you take advantage of the possibilities?"

3. **Advocate for and provide a means for the company to, through EAPs and compassionate input and feedback, support those seeking access to counseling or other related services.**

4. **After six months, and again after a year, conduct another anonymous poll to identify employees' sense of impact on their lives and job performance. You can also assess impact in other ways, such as improved management, productivity, and the bottom line.**

If people are indeed our most precious resource, and if children grow up needing support to be the best they can be, and you want to be a part of that for the benefit of all, including your business, your action is needed.

"You got this," as we say. Gimme a holler if you want some help!

Pamela J. Pine, PhD, MPH, is an international speaker and health, development, and communication professional who has dedicated her career to supporting underserved populations in over 30 countries. Since 2000, her work has centered on childhood trauma and protection, with a particular focus on preventing and addressing child sexual abuse (CSA), trafficking, and other adverse childhood experiences (ACEs).

As Founder and former CEO of Stop the Silence® – Stop Child Sexual Abuse, Inc., Dr. Pine established a leading voice in advocacy, education, training, and other trauma-informed programming. Since 2021, she has directed Stop the Silence®, now a Department of the Institute on Violence, Abuse and Trauma (IVAT), where she continues advancing prevention, education, training, and empowerment strategies for individuals, families, communities, and organizations worldwide.

In addition to her public health and nonprofit leadership, Dr. Pine is a professor, best-selling author (among her chapters in 12 collaborative books are *Stop the Silence® – Thriving After Child Sexual Abuse* and a chapter for parents to read to children to communicate about abuse in *Brave Kids Vol. 3*), poet, award-winning photographer, and multimedia artist. She integrates creative expression—through painting, music, and writing—into her work as a means of opening hearts and minds to the realities of trauma and the possibilities of healing.

A recognized global advocate, Dr. Pine and her work have been featured on NBC, CNN, PBS, and iHeart Radio, and in publications such as *The Washington Post*, *The Washington Times*, and *On Purpose Women's Magazine*. Her awards include a Lifetime Advocacy Achievement Award in 2017 from IVAT, the International Leadership Women's Impact Award (2024), and, in 2025, she was honored with the Voices of Courage Award® for her lifetime commitment to protecting children and preventing abuse worldwide.

Connect with Pamela:

Websites: https://www.ivatcenters.org/stop-the-silence
https://www.drpamelajpine.com/

LinkedIn: https://www.linkedin.com/in/pamelajpine/

CHAPTER 4

STOP DOING EVERYONE ELSE'S WORK

HOW SETTING BOUNDARIES GIVES YOU PURPOSE

Heather Archer, M.A.

*"Time is more valuable than money.
You can get more money, but you cannot get more time."*

- Jim Rohn

MY STORY

My mother never hesitated to tell me what to do when a task needed to be completed. She neither asked nor invited. It was simply understood that I'd stop whatever I was doing and complete the task, her way, immediately. This lack of autonomy created low self-respect, and it was completely invisible to me; I couldn't have told you I had a problem, but I did.

When I went off to college and later entered the job market, I started to understand the effect this low self-respect had on me. Not believing I had the option to say yes or no to a task someone else needed to have completed paved the way for me to be an "Easy Yes Person."

"Hey Heather, would you mind editing this report for me?" asked a co-worker.

"I would love to," I respond without giving a second thought, already starting to feel fatigued.

"Can you organize the lunch for our team meeting?" my boss asked me.

"Sure, I can do that," I answered, cringing on the inside as I said it.

"Someone needs to work with the summer interns to get them onboarded. Heather, you good to do that again this year?" the HR Manager asked.

"Absolutely!" I answered, reigniting the simmering resentment from last year.

Once I realized I was an "Easy Yes Person," I could no longer hide from it. I was keenly aware of when I did things that weren't a good use of either my time or my energy.

Unfortunately, while I was aware of the problem, I didn't have the skills or confidence to diplomatically decline the tasks others wanted me to do. I continued saying yes, which led to a growing resentment. Every ask that came in made my body tense up. I was irritable and always seemed to be bitter about everything. *Why am I always getting these jobs dumped on me? Why can't I say no like everyone else seems to?*

I wasn't always the best person to work with. This also led to my being disengaged from the work and the mission of the company that employed me, which was not good for my future either.

As I matured, I gained both the confidence and the diplomacy to guard my time and energy. The result is the ability to say no when a task doesn't serve me, but saying it diplomatically so that my *no* doesn't damage my relationships and the work I do.

I feel a lightness when I walk away from the things that don't serve me. I breathe easier and look forward with enthusiasm to the work I've agreed to do.

"Hey Heather, would you mind editing this report for me?" asked a co-worker.

"No, I don't have the expertise to offer valuable edits on this topic," I calmly responded.

"Can you organize the lunch for our team meeting?" my boss asked.

"John is a master at ordering group lunches. I'll give him the details for our meeting and let him do his thing," I answered, firmly redirecting the task to the appropriate person.

"Someone needs to work with the summer interns to get them onboarded. Heather, you good to do that again this year?" the HR manager asked.

"I am happy to act as a resource, but I don't have the bandwidth right now for a greater role in that project," I reply, quietly sighing with relief as I step away from a task that haunted me for years.

THE ASK

I now understand that the problem wasn't with the people asking me to help. People are always going to ask. This is because there will always be tasks people don't want to do, and it's a natural human inclination to try to unload them on others. It's sort of like an adult version of the Hot Potato game we used to play as kids during recess. If you never played that game, here's the most important rule: the loser is the one left holding the ball at the end. Everyone else wins.

So if the problem wasn't with the asker, that meant the problem was with me and my inability to politely but firmly set boundaries around how I spent my time and energy.

I couldn't set proper boundaries, and I blamed others for my shortcomings.

Fast forward to becoming an entrepreneur in 2017. Now that I found myself in charge of my own time and financial success, fear entered the picture. It convinced me that saying no to any client and/or project, no matter how outside of my expertise it may be, wasn't an option. I had to say yes to everything. I had to take on every client and every task.

Fear did this by playing on my deepest, secret fear: being homeless.

Let me be very clear here: when I say "being homeless," I don't mean eventually. Fear worked hard to convince me that I'd be homeless tomorrow. If today is Monday, it told me: *You'll wake without a home on Tuesday morning.* Sounds ridiculous when you say it like that, I know. But that's the trick to fear. It can make the ridiculous sound quite rational.

Here is the thing about emotions—they can only live, only exist, when they're being felt. The thing about fear, specifically, is that when it's doing its job of keeping you safe, it becomes the hero and the decision maker. Fear loves to be the hero and to be in control. It will create opportunities to do both. Enter my impractical fear of being homeless.

Fear recognized the perfect storm of elements: my "Yes, I'd love to help" upbringing, my fear of losing my home, and my life as an entrepreneur. Then it knitted them together, guiding me to say yes to every potential client, project, and task.

Needless to say, the first few years of being on my own were very rough. Then I started to really lean into valuing my time and energy more than the moments of discomfort when fear tried to be in charge. I started small, saying no to opportunities that weren't a good fit or that I knew I couldn't do well.

Guess what? My mortgage still got paid!

I realized I had more time to say yes to the things I love doing and am good at, which brought more work. While I took this journey, I discovered that I wasn't alone.

There are many reasons why we say yes when we want to say no, but the end result is the same: we become overworked, resentful, stressed, and unfocused. To help others find the confidence I did, and learn the skills needed to set and hold to those boundaries, I created The Promotion Equation™ program.

The Promotion Equation™ crystallized when two things collided in my world. The first was when I read the book *The No Club* (Linda Babcock). I highly recommend it. The second was when I started coaching my adult daughter, Lexi. She started a new corporate job and, within a month, was already complaining. "I am so busy throughout the day, but I don't know what I have actually done all day," she said.

Turns out she was busy doing other people's work because they asked the new person in the office for help, hoping she'd say yes, and she did, without question, hesitation, or even considering how it would affect her own work. She fell for the myth of "Be a team player by helping others out, and you'll get ahead."

Sadly, it doesn't work that way. You just get asked to help more often.

So many of us do this, and it sets up a very dangerous precedent—we become the "Easy Yes Person" in the office, on the team, and in the family.

Here is the secret no one wants you to know: Just because someone asks for our help doesn't mean we are required or obligated to give it. Once you recognize that you're spending too much of your time doing other people's work, you're at the starting gate of your journey to find more time in your day and more energy for the things you value at work and in life.

THE PAUSE

One of the simplest, but not easiest, ways to turn this situation around is to learn to pause before giving your answer when someone asks you to help them or to complete a task.

I've worked as a workshop facilitator for over 30 years, and one of the best lessons I learned, thankfully early in my career, was the power of the pause. It's amazingly helpful in so many situations. Unfortunately, people are afraid of providing even a moment of silence in a conversation.

Using a pause when someone is asking you to do something for them has great power, and that power resides with you. Being able to sit in silence, for even just a few seconds, is something a confident person does. It says you're willing to take the time to think your way through your answer and not be rushed. It says you value your time and will give a well-thought-out answer. An answer they're not likely to be able to change.

Besides showing your confidence, pauses give you real time to make an intentional decision about the ask. Pausing can also help those of us who say yes too quickly. It builds in time to start breaking the yes habit.

If the ask is in a group setting, your pause gives someone else the chance to speak up and ask a question or volunteer.

Big task or little task—the only difference is the length of the pause. The length of the pause is in direct proportion to the task being discussed. A quick, brief task ("Can you run to the Copy Center and pick up those workbooks for tomorrow's class?") might only need a three to five-second pause and then your answer. A bigger task ("We would love to have you join the holiday party planning committee. It would be a three-month-long project.") warrants a longer pause, maybe even up to a week. The immediate response after a short pause would be "Thank you for asking. Let me think about it, and I will get back to you next week with my decision."

Pausing can be awkward when you first start. What you really need is something to occupy your brain during those few moments. Something you can repeat until you have sorted your next step. You need a *pause mantra*.

A *pause mantra* is a short, positive statement that you repeat, silently, that fills the time between asking and answering. For more information on creating your own *pause mantra*, see the Tool section of this chapter.

"Hey Heather, would you mind editing this report for me?" asked a co-worker.

There's silence as I think to myself: *I'm feeling really awkward with the silence but doing it anyway!*

"No, I don't have the expertise to offer valuable edits on this topic," I calmly respond, feeling confident and grounded in my response.

"Can you organize the lunch for our team meeting?" my boss asked.

Shhhh. Wait for it. Wait for it. Just wait.

"John is a master at ordering group lunches. I will give him the details for our meeting and let him do his thing," I answer, using that moment of silence to find a way to help without owning the task.

"Someone needs to work with the summer interns to get them onboarded. Heather, you good to do that again this year?" the HR Manager asks.

We are just listening right now, not speaking.

"I am happy to act as a resource, but I do not have the bandwidth right now for a greater role in that project," I reply, quietly sighing with relief at not having taken on that burden again.

YOUR ANSWER

Once you've had the time to clearly think through the task being offered, you can determine your answer. Your answer is flexible according to any given day and time. What you're really looking for is the right answer for you, right now. You might have said yes to that ask yesterday, but today you cannot. You might be able to say yes tomorrow, but you'll have to wait and see what tomorrow brings.

Each ask must be judged in its own moment, not according to what you have done in the past. This will be hard for the asker to hear, as they're coming to you as their "Easy Yes Person," and now they're hearing something else. This is where the respect is built—in stating and sticking to your boundaries.

You have three choices when you finally answer:

1. Say Yes: You can say yes whenever it serves you, but remember, you are trying to be intentional with all your answers.

2. Say Yes with Modifications: Once you have had a moment to consider the task, you might find that some modifications would move it from not serving you to serving you.

3. Say No: Let's talk about how to say no and diplomatically decline tasks that do not serve you.

Your goal is to give your answer without damaging the relationship. Be sure to respond as soon as you have made your decision. Otherwise, the ask will still distract and weigh on you. It doesn't get easier the longer you wait, so don't wait. I now find a moment of relief after giving my no answer.

Here are some techniques to help you craft your diplomatic decline:

- Be clear and direct when you decline.
- Find the yes in the no.
- Provide the asker with the tools.
- Offer to cross-train someone.

Here are a few of my favorite diplomatic declines:

- "No. Thank you for asking."
- "I can introduce you to [NAME]. I have found them to be very helpful."
- "I can do this but first, what other task/project should I deprioritize?"
- "No, I need to prioritize my current workload right now."

If you find this difficult to do in person, and the task lends itself to it, you can move the conversation to some form of written communication: text, email, etc.: "Thank you for asking. I will send you an email with my answer later today."

AND THEN WHAT

Once you have delivered your diplomatic decline, you need to minimize the conversational space the asker has to try to pressure you into changing your answer. You can do this in a variety of ways:

- Distract–Ask them a question on an unrelated topic.
- Distance–End the conversation and walk away, or do not respond to the next email/text.
- Deflect–Gently steer away from the topic without engaging it directly.
- Disrupt–Interrupt the pattern by introducing a new boundary or unexpected shift.

So, where am I on my journey? Not at the end. I still say yes when I should've said no, usually because I forgot to pause and really think about the ask.

When I make that mistake, I either complete the task (without resentment now) or I let the asker know that I really will not be able to help them after all. Both are just painful enough to remind me not to skip that very important step of pausing in the future.

To end my daughter Lexi's story, she has become a badass at saying no. She says it to me all the time and has even diplomatically declined requests from the Senior Vice President of her organization, and they respected her for it! Lexi moved from being just a task completer to a valued strategic partner.

If you find yourself falling prey to the "yes habit," then pausing, even for a few seconds, can have great power, but it can also feel awkward at first. Keep reading to learn how to create your own, personalized *pause mantra*.

THE TOOL

The most important part of the pause is the silence; resist the urge to fill it. It's important not to appear uncomfortable.

A *pause mantra* is a short, positive statement that fills the time between ask and answer.

Here are some guidelines for creating your own:

- Keep it short and simple.
- Make it true for you.
- Make it either positive or neutral.
- It can be whimsical and nonsensical.

Here are a few samples:

- *We're just listening right now, not speaking.*
- *God grant me your wisdom to say no when appropriate…time after time.*
- *I will earn respect by setting boundaries on my time and work.*
- *Time is a gift, and this isn't my giving season.*

To go along with the *pause mantra*, you can also add an action to help with the silence. Here are some ideas:

- Take a slow drink or bite of food.
- Take a few calm, deep breaths.
- Look at the person as if waiting for more information.
- Think of a question.

Pausing before you commit is a power move, and you're absolutely capable of making it a habit. That tiny moment of breathing room helps you check the request against your goals, spot the distractions disguised as "quick favors," and choose what truly deserves your energy. You're not hesitating–you're leading with intention and protecting your focus. You got this.

Heather Archer, M.A., is the Founder and Principal at Training de Jour and is the creator of The Promotion Equation™, a practical framework that helps people spot and diplomatically decline non-promotable work so they can focus on what truly matters and moves their careers forward. With over 30 years in the corporate world, she's seen how easily talented professionals–especially women–get buried under tasks that don't lead to advancement. Her work is all about changing that.

Her motto is: "The more we laugh, the better we learn and grow." The number of times she's been asked where she performs stand-up comedy proves she lives this motto in every keynote presentation and workshop (though no, she doesn't do stand-up). Her ability to find the human and the humor, even in "hard" topics, helps participants engage more fully with the material and each other.

She is a self-confessed afternoon tea aficionado who loves visiting new tea rooms everywhere she goes.

Want help increasing your pausing skill? Download the free **Pausing with Confidence** worksheet at: https://trainingdejour.com/free/pause

Interested in bringing this topic to your workplace? Let's connect and see what that can look like.

Connect with Heather:

Email: heather@trainingdejour.com

Website: https://trainingdejour.com/promotion-equation/

LinkedIn: https://www.linkedin.com/in/heatherarcher/

Innovation Women: https://speaker.innovationwomen.com/user/20217

All American Entertainment:
https://www.allamericanspeakers.com/speakers/467436/Heather-Archer

CHAPTER 5

THE BEAUTY OF THE BLOW UP

HOW MOMENTS THAT BREAK YOU WORK FOR YOU

Laura Reynolds, PCC

MY STORY

For years after my divorce, I lived out of bags, not because I was traveling, not because I was nomadic or adventurous or free. I lived out of bags because I didn't trust that anything in my life was permanent anymore. Drawers felt too committed. Hangers felt aspirational. Closets—real closets—felt like promises I wasn't ready to make.

So I floated. I kept things folded neatly inside duffels and overnight bags, stacked against walls or tucked under beds, always half-packed, always ready to leave. *It's practical*, I told myself. *It's flexible. It's easier.* But the truth was quieter and heavier: living out of bags allowed me to avoid deciding who I was now.

Because deciding meant letting go. And letting go meant touching things I wasn't sure I could survive touching.

My closet—when I finally let myself open it—wasn't just full. It was crowded in a way that felt oppressive, almost accusatory. The door barely opened without resistance, as if the contents inside were bracing themselves against escape. Every inch was occupied by something from a former life, or several former lives layered on top of one another like sediment.

There was my wedding dress, still wrapped carefully in plastic, still white, still pristine, still holding the weight of a promise that once felt sacred and inevitable and was now neither. I moved it from house to house, year to year, telling myself: *You'll decide what to do with it someday. Someday* was a word I used often. Someday was how I postponed grief.

There were bins of high school spirit wear—t-shirts and hoodies emblazoned with school colors and mascots, saved for no logical reason except the quiet, irrational fear that I might one day need them. *What if there's another spirit day? What if my daughter needs one?* What if getting rid of them meant admitting that chapter was officially closed?

There were jeans that were "in style" at some point, bought because someone else wore them well, because a magazine told me they were flattering, because I thought if I just tried harder, I'd feel confident in them. I hated every single pair. I never reached for them. But I kept them anyway, as if discomfort itself was a form of discipline.

There were dresses I wore for other people. Sweaters tied to memories that weren't even mine, gifts given with expectation, obligation, or unspoken meaning. Clothes that fit a version of me who existed primarily to make others comfortable, impressed, and reassured.

My closet was not storage, it was a museum of selves I no longer inhabited.

And every time I stood in front of it, deciding what to wear, I felt the same low-grade anxiety rise in my chest. My shoulders tightened. My breathing became shallow. I reached for the safest thing, the most neutral, least expressive option- and moved on with my day without ever asking what I wanted to feel like in my body.

I didn't yet have language for it, but I lived in a constant state of self-abandonment.

Around this same time, I began to build my business.

On paper, everything made sense. I had experience, credentials, and a vision. I knew what I wanted to create and who I wanted to serve. I'd done harder things than this before. And yet nothing felt fluid. Everything required effort that bordered on force.

I pushed constantly. I pushed for clarity, for momentum, and for confidence. I pushed myself to show up online, to speak boldly, to claim space that didn't yet feel like it belonged to me.

You're stuck because you need a better strategy. You need a clearer niche or a sharper brand, more time, more rest, more courage, I told myself.

But late at night, standing barefoot on my bedroom floor, staring into the chaos of my closet, I felt a different truth whispering underneath all of that noise.

You can't move forward while you're still living with every version of who you used to be.

I avoided the closet the way people avoid difficult conversations. I knew it mattered. I knew it was waiting. *You'll get to it once things settle down,* I kept telling myself.

But nothing settles down when you're building something new.

Eventually, the avoidance started to feel louder than the task itself. The closet became symbolic in a way I couldn't ignore. Every time I hesitated before making a decision in my business—before raising my rates, before speaking my truth, before trusting my instincts—I felt the same sensation I felt standing in front of those overstuffed hangers: Overwhelm. Confusion. Constriction.

One afternoon, after yet another day of spinning my wheels, I sat on the edge of my bed and let myself be honest.

I am not stuck because I don't know what to do.

I'm stuck because I'm afraid of who I'll be once I do it.

I realized that I framed the closet all wrong. I told myself what I didn't want to experience: the mess, the emotion, the time it would take, the decisions, the grief. I rehearsed the discomfort over and over, convincing myself it would be unbearable.

So instead, I tried something different. I asked myself: *How do you want to feel when it's done?*

Not what the closet would look like, but who I would be standing in front of it.

I wanted to feel light, unburdened, and clear. I wanted to open the door without flinching. I wanted to get dressed without negotiating with my past. I wanted to recognize myself again. And once I named that version of me, something shifted.

I didn't start by purging. I didn't start by pulling things out and reliving memories. I started by deciding who I was becoming.

I feverishly purchased a rolling wardrobe rack, the kind you see backstage at fashion shows, metal and unapologetic, designed to be seen. It felt bold, temporary, and intentional.

Then I did something I never allowed myself to do before: I chose clothes based on alignment instead of aspiration.

I found five full outfits from style bloggers whose energy resonated with me, not because I wanted to be them, but because when I looked at those outfits, I felt a sense of recognition—relief, like my body exhaled.

I bought everything—the tops, the pants, the jackets, the shoes, the accessories. I didn't overthink it. I didn't bargain with myself. I let desire lead.

When the packages arrived, I lined those outfits up on the rolling rack like a declaration.

This is who I'm choosing to be.

Then I made a rule so simple it felt almost laughable.

If it doesn't align with these outfits, it's out.

No debates. No "just in case." No sentimental loopholes.

I opened my closet and began.

At first, my hands shook. I moved slowly, deliberately, pulling items off hangers one by one. Each piece carried a weight I hadn't fully acknowledged before. Some were heavy with grief. Others with resentment. Others with an obligation.

The wedding dress came first.

I stood holding it longer than I expected. The fabric was still soft. Still beautiful. And for a moment, I felt the familiar ache, the mourning of what had been, the life I thought I was building when I wore it.

But then something surprising happened. I didn't feel sadness. I felt gratitude.

That dress represented a version of me who believed in love deeply enough to commit her whole self to it. A version of me who hoped, who trusted, who showed up fully.

She wasn't foolish. She was brave.

And I didn't need to keep the dress to honor her.

I folded it carefully, placed it into a bag, and felt my shoulders drop. Piece by piece, the closet emptied.

Spirit wear—gone. Jeans I hated—gone. Dresses I wore to please other people—gone. Clothes tied to expectations that were never mine to carry—gone.

Ten trash bags filled the room.

As the pile grew, something else happened inside my body. My chest felt more open, and my breathing was deeper. I noticed sensations I hadn't noticed in years—a lightness in my spine, a softness in my jaw.

When the closet was finally empty, it echoed.

I stood in the doorway and cried. Not the kind of crying that comes from devastation, but the kind that comes from relief, from release, from finally telling the truth.

I rolled the new wardrobe into place and hung the five outfits with care. Everything had space. Everything belonged.

For the first time in years, my closet reflected my present instead of my past. And that's when I realized something that stopped me in my tracks.

My body had been living in that crowded closet.

Every old identity I kept hanging there was something I still carried internally. Every "just in case" outfit mirrored a "just in case" belief. Every item I kept for someone else represented a choice I still made out of obligation instead of alignment.

Letting go of the clothes let go of the weight.

In the weeks that followed, my business began to change in ways I couldn't have predicted. I spoke more clearly. I made decisions faster. I trusted myself without spiraling. Opportunities flowed with less resistance. Conversations felt more honest. My work felt more like an extension of who I was instead of something I had to manufacture.

I wasn't trying to become someone new. I was finally making room for the person I already was.

The closet didn't change my life because it became neat, organized, or aesthetically pleasing. It changed my life because it became truthful.

And truth—when you let it breathe—has a way of rearranging everything.

I now understand that we don't get stuck because we don't know what to do.

We get stuck because we're still living with versions of ourselves that have already served their purpose.

Sometimes, the bravest thing you can do is open the door, take a breath, and let them go.

THE TOOL

When the closet was finally quiet—when the hangers had room to breathe, and the weight of old versions of me had lifted—I understood something clearly:

The real work wasn't just in what I removed. **It was in what I chose next.**

Because clearing space is only the beginning, living in alignment with who you are becoming is the practice that follows.

What we wear is one of the most intimate decisions we make each day. It's the first agreement we make with our body. The first signal we send to ourselves about who we are allowed to be.

When chosen intentionally, clothing becomes more than fabric. It becomes feedback. That's where this method begins.

What you wear elevates how you feel, and how you feel shapes how you move through your life.

Before touching a hanger or folding a single item, start here:

STEP ONE: NAME THE FEELING

Choose one specific outfit—something you wear often or want to wear more intentionally.

Ask yourself:

What three things do I want to feel about myself when I put this on?

Not how you want to look. Not how you want others to see you. But how you want to **feel in your body.**

Is it confident? Is it clear, free, steady, bold, or badass?

Write your three words down. Let them guide you.

THE **CREATE** METHOD

This method isn't about minimalism or rules. I'm not about to have you Marie Condo your closet! It's about alignment. It's about giving yourself permission to move from the chapter you were in to the chapter you feel called to now.

C-CLARITY

How do I want to feel today and who am I becoming long-term?

Clarity begins with honesty.

Ask yourself:

- How do I want to feel when I walk into a room?
- How do I want to feel when I make decisions?
- How do I want to feel in my own skin?

Your closet should support the future you- not negotiate with the past.

R-RITUAL

What helps me shift when I feel off?

Getting dressed doesn't have to feel heavy or frustrating. If you let it, it can almost be a sort of grounding ritual.

Ritual might look like:

- Choosing clothes the night before
- Pausing to breathe before getting dressed

- Playing music that matches the energy you want (go ahead…dance!)
- Changing outfits intentionally when your mood shifts

Ritual teaches your nervous system that it's safe to change.

E-EDITING

Turn your closet into a library of how you want to feel.

Release "just in case" thinking.

Ask each item:

- Does this support how I want to feel?
- Does this reflect who I am now?
- Do I feel more like myself when I wear this?

Your closet is not an archive of who you were. It's a collection of who you're becoming.

A-ALIGNMENT

Notice how details affect your energy.

Clothing sends a message before words do, especially to you.

Pay attention to:

- **Color** and how it shifts your mood
- **Proportion** and how it affects confidence
- **Texture** and how it comforts your body
- **Structure vs. softness** and how you hold yourself

Alignment is learning your language, not following trends.

T-TRUTH

Tell the story of who you are now.

Every outfit tells a story.

Ask:

- Is this a story I still believe?
- Am I wearing this for myself or for someone else?
- Does this feel honest in this season of my life?

Truth doesn't need to be dramatic. It only needs to be real.

E-EXPANSION

Choose growth again and again.

You will continue to evolve.

Your closet should evolve with you.

Expansion means:

- Letting go when something no longer fits, physically or emotionally
- Making room for new expressions of yourself
- Trusting that growth doesn't erase who you were, it builds on it

Clearing out your closet doesn't mean you're losing something. It means you're ready. Ready to stop carrying versions of yourself that no longer belong to this season. Ready to stop living in proof of who you used to be.

Becoming often looks like release before it looks like arrival.

This is not the end of who you were.

It's the beginning of who you always knew you could be.

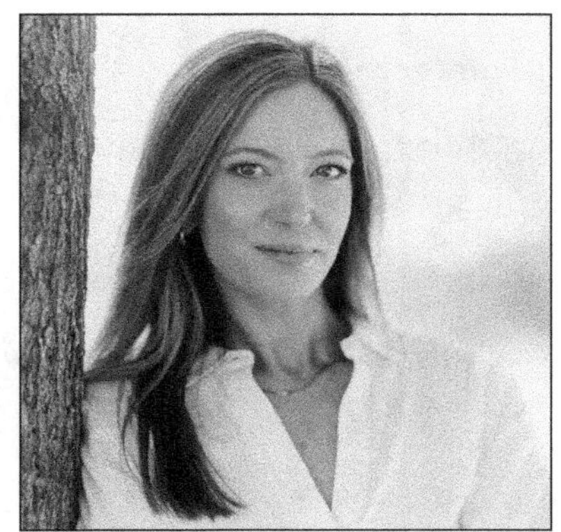 **Laura Reynolds** is the Founder and CEO of **Executive Endurance Coaching, LLC**, where she helps leaders move out of survival mode and into sustained, intentional performance. With over 14 years of experience as a recruiter, hiring manager, and talent acquisition consultant, Laura has supported leaders and teams at organizations including Meta, ZeroFox, and Johns Hopkins. Her background gives her a rare, inside understanding of what leadership actually demands in high-stakes, high-growth, and mission-driven environments.

Laura is a Professional Certified Coach (PCC) through the International Coaching Federation, and her work blends evidence-based leadership development with an endurance mindset rooted in clarity, resilience, and consistency. Before stepping fully into coaching, she spent years sitting on both sides of the hiring table- building talent strategies, advising executives, and helping shape teams and cultures. She knows the pressure leaders face because she has lived it.

Beyond her coaching practice, Laura is the host of **The Grit Files**, a podcast exploring real stories of resilience, growth, and what it takes to sustain performance through life's hardest seasons. She is also a multi-time ultramarathon and triathlon competitor, embodying the endurance principles she teaches: clarity beats chaos, consistency beats intensity, and mindset determines everything.

Above all, Laura is a proud mom to an incredible seven-year-old daughter, whose presence continually grounds her work in what matters most. Through her coaching, writing, and speaking, Laura helps people remember who they are, dismantle the stories holding them back, and build the mental and strategic foundations needed to thrive—one intentional step at a time.

Connect with Laura:

LinkedIn: https://www.linkedin.com/in/laura-leeb-reynolds/

Instagram: https://www.instagram.com/executive_endurance_coaching/
https://www.instagram.com/the.gritfiles/

Email: LReynolds2124@outlook.com

CHAPTER 6

CONFIDENT ENOUGH TO ASK

QUESTIONS ARE THE MARK OF COURAGE AND HUMILITY

Agnes M. Geisler, HRMP

MY STORY

It's just too risky to ask that question.

I stared at the whiteboard in front of us in Sagamore, our largest staff meeting room in the building, as a colleague paced back and forth, fidgeting with the dry-erase marker in his hand.

For years, I dreamed of sitting with these leaders, on this team—the executive leadership team of our growing church. Not because I idolize the team and the role, but because I truly believe I have something to offer to help our church reach people with the grace and truth Jesus offers. And here we were—at an inflection point—as our founding pastor had announced his resignation. He would move back to his home state of Kentucky and into a new pastoral leadership role at his home church.

With this major organizational change in front of us, we know the makeup of our executive team will change from how it currently looks. We need to add new players and shift players around into different roles. But how do we define the types of skills necessary for this team?

As the only woman on the team and the newest member, I felt like I was still finding my place and my voice. Everyone else had been on the team for years longer than I and built camaraderie amongst themselves as a cohesive unit. Here I was trying to find my place. Thoughts, questions, and insecurities swirled in my head often, causing my chest to feel heavy, my jaw to clench, and more words than necessary to come out of my mouth. Being the newest part of the team, I'd always wonder if my contributions were actually helpful. Was I talking too much or not enough? Was I too "in the weeds" about areas of ministry and missing the big picture? Do I have a pulse on the right things? The questions I'd ask myself in my head felt endless.

In many vision-focused, innovative conversations we'd have as a team, I felt like the odd one out, not naturally wired to think creatively but rather more systems-oriented. It felt like everyone else could flex that innovative, dreaming muscle a lot more naturally than I, and I was dead weight in the room. I left those meetings feeling completely exhausted and useless. Those conversations were not my element, whereas everyone else seemed to thrive and come alive. I'm in awe of people whose minds work in that way, constantly imagining the "what ifs" and dreaming of what could be years down the line. I can listen to someone's ideas and build off of them, but creating something from nothing was such a foreign concept to me.

My mind just does not work that way. And in those meetings, during those kinds of conversations, I felt like the runt of the litter, trying hard to keep up.

As we listed attributes on the whiteboard, I felt that familiar heaviness on my chest start to pile on. My cheeks flushed as I considered my insecurity, and my brain rapidly fired:

Is visionary, creative innovation an attribute needed on this team?

That's not my strength. I don't think I'm good at that at all.

If they say it is, and it's not a strength of mine, will that be my ticket off this team?

It's just too risky to ask that question.

I considered in that moment what was at risk if I brought that up.

Will I draw attention to something no one else really noticed, but now that I mentioned it, they'll realize it actually is a non-negotiable?

Is it time for me to accept that this role just isn't for me?

As we talked back and forth, debating on nuances and verbiage, I realized it was time for me to make my own decision.

"I have a question."

Carl, Jonathan, and Mike all turned towards me simultaneously. Sarah, our lead pastor's executive assistant, paused what she was doing. The clicking of her keyboard stopped, her hands lowered, and her gaze lifted up from her laptop. All eyes were on me—undivided attention.

Oh man. This is it. No turning back now.

I took a breath (not too deep that they could sense my nervousness), calmed myself, and started to speak.

"Is it a 'requirement' to be a more visionary-type leader? I'm not really the innovative, dreaming type. It's not a strength of mine, but it is definitely a strength for the rest of you. And I just don't know if that's something that's a deal breaker for being on this team."

What is wild is that I don't remember how the rest of the conversation went (even though ultimately it was shared that this trait was *not* a requirement). What I remember is building up the courage to simply ask the question that could've gone either way.

It took guts.

I was scared.

It was risky.

But taking a deep breath and asking the question gave me confidence.

I realized that what was standing in my way was **me**. I was courageous enough to say the scary thing out loud, to not let fear and uncertainty call the shots in my head anymore, and just **ask the question**.

What was standing in my way was the idea that asking questions showed weakness: If you didn't know something, then you weren't the smartest person in the room. And if you weren't the smartest person in the room, why would anyone listen to you?

I don't think anyone ever explicitly told me these things, but I learned them along the way as a college graduate in my first "big girl job" working for Target as an Executive Team Leader, leading a surprise visit for high-level corporate leaders at my store. Whoever was the Leader-on-Duty was responsible for leading any store visit, and all eyes were on you. If you didn't have the answers to their questions, you made everyone look bad—your Store Team Leader, your colleagues, your entire store.

I learned that I was good at saying a whole lot and sounding smart, elaborating enough to give a "good enough" response. My external persona could be turned on at the flip of a switch, while, internally, I was nervous I would be "found out" as not knowledgeable enough, strong enough, confident enough… a good-enough leader.

You were expected to know the answer on the spot, right away. As a result, I internalized: *Questions are a sign of weakness*. And you better believe I wasn't going to do anything that would make someone think I was weak.

That day, sitting in Sagamore, when I dug up the courage to ask the question, it felt like it unlocked a part of me finally willing to dip her toe in the water while someone stood next to me who could've pushed me in at any moment, without warning, and trusting that they wouldn't.

Everyone is wired differently, and it's a beautiful thing. When different people bring their different strengths to the table, the possibilities are endless. I have a keen sense of how things fit together, how to bring systems, structure, and clarity to a process. But if I'm not careful, I can come in with all the answers, tell people what to do, and not ask questions to learn, discover, and equip them to lead.

Fast forward six months, and I began working with an executive leadership coach. We identify one area of growth for me is to move from a *command and control* approach of leadership to a *coach* approach. While having all the answers may be nice, it doesn't help others grow and learn for themselves; it unintentionally conditions people I lead to bring problems to me instead of empowering them to find solutions.

We brought a new kids' ministry director onto our team who brought extensive professional experience to the table but had never worked in a church ministry context before. So many of the job specifics were new to her. Natasha brought a list of questions asking for guidance on how to address those situations in our routine one-on-ones.

Given my years of experience working in ministry, it was easy for me to draw on my experience to simply say, "Oh, yeah, I've had something similar happen before. Here's what you can do," and give her the play-by-play. However, through this personal leadership coaching, we uncovered that the best leaders *coach* their people to think for themselves, problem-solve, and get their own hands dirty.

But if I'm honest, I *like* being the leader who has all the answers! I feel like I *am* helping when they learn from my mistakes and don't waste time. But I rob others of their own growth by not challenging them directly, asking questions for them to discover what's next and best.

Natasha continued to bring her questions, and I began to shift my response to, "Well, what do you think?" She'd crack a small smirk that showed her slight annoyance that I just asked her a question right back, and then she'd share her thoughts and perspective. She knew I meant well, yet wasn't going to give her the easy way out! She was, and is, a capable leader and was often already heading in the right direction! As she shared, I listened intently, nodding along as I understood what she said and then responded by affirming the direction she was heading, sharing some cautions to consider or ways I've taken similar action, and learnings I had as a result that she could keep in mind.

It was a constant humility gut-check to not just tell her what to do, but to ask a question back and walk alongside her as *she* led.

Questions are exposing, in a lot of different ways. Questions can expose what you don't currently know, what you actually do know but are hesitant to take action on, and gaps, misunderstandings, assumptions, and confusion. Questions highlight both what is known and what is unknown that needs to become known.

More often than not, rather than asking questions to gain clarity or expose the knowns *and* unknowns, I instead trudge through the confusion and simply untangle things myself. I was working harder and not smarter.

In my mind, asking questions meant I didn't have the answer. I didn't want to be exposed for not knowing the answer. The judgments loudly played in my head:

How long have you worked here, and you still don't know that?

Everyone knows that Agnes, why don't you?

It's not as big a deal as you're making it out to be.

Don't get too much in the weeds.

If you're asking about that, what else are you unsure of?

I can't control what people think of me, but I can control how I act in the room, and if I didn't ask the question, they didn't have to question the kind of leader I am.

It took a long time to realize that asking questions wasn't a sign of weakness, but actually confidence.

Confidence that you're willing to put yourself out there and be exposed for what you may not know yet.

Confidence in yourself as a person that you could gain new information that may change how you approach entirely, perhaps even making some prior work obsolete. And I never want to waste time, so I would stay away from that like the plague!

Confidence that you're willing to do the work to dig in deep, pull on threads, and see what unravels.

And in a beautiful way, alongside confidence is humility. As you ask questions, you realize that while whatever unravels may be scary and expose even more (and possibly bigger) problems, you are willing to pull on the thread and see what happens.

I don't want to follow a hesitant leader or a know-it-all, but rather a wise, discerning, humble leader who elevates others.

And if I want to lead others, I also have to take courageous steps forward, wisely and confidently. When I ask a question or turn in a certain direction that may not be the best, I can't let my confidence take a hit, and it turns into timidity or arrogance (both sides of the same coin). Rather, I want to be a humble leader, willing to take ownership of my decisions, course-correct, and keep moving forward. I want to be a humble leader who doesn't just tell people what to do but uses questions to elevate others in how they think, act, and lead.

The best way to discern what *is* the best direction to go in isn't by knowing everything, but by asking questions—not just any question, but the wise questions worth fighting for and asking, because of what might be uncovered in the process of answering.

But there are a million questions you could ask. Oftentimes, as leaders, we have to help those we lead take wise steps back to gain perspective and ensure the direction we take is the right one. So, what questions do we even ask? I believe five simple words can remind us of six key questions that will bring clarity and confidence as we lead, problem solve, and innovate.

THE TOOL

Whether you're tackling a brand new problem or feel like you're swimming in the deep end and don't know how you got there, there are five words that lead to six questions that can help you gain clarity and define what it is you want to run after and achieve.

I've used this framework when working with leaders who know something needs to change, when something feels off but they can't quite identify what needs to change, or when they're challenged to tackle a newly identified or suspected problem.

WHO, WHAT, HOW, WHY, WIN

Who is this for?

What is the problem we're trying to solve?

What are we doing?

How are we going to do it?

Why are we doing this?

Win → How do we measure success?

Let's dive a little deeper into each of these questions:

WHO IS THIS FOR?

Who is going to be impacted, both directly and indirectly?

If you're unclear about your audience, you won't know who your target is or learn how to best communicate with that audience.

WHAT IS THE PROBLEM WE'RE TRYING TO SOLVE?

Don't simply problem-solve. It's easy to solve a problem. It's harder to step back and determine what exactly is the problem that we're trying to solve. Pull on the thread and discover what's at the core of the issue coming up.

WHAT ARE WE DOING?

Boil down your action into one to two sentences max. Based on the problem you're trying to solve, what action are you taking to solve the problem? There likely are multiple steps you'll take to solve the problem, but you have to be confident in what you will do to solve the problem you've identified. If you aren't clear, everyone else will, in turn, be confused and timid.

HOW ARE WE GOING TO DO IT?

This is your nuts and bolts of what exactly you are going to do to tackle this situation. Don't get too technical and in the weeds in your "how", but you do need to articulate the action steps you're taking to solve the problem you've identified. Later on, you'll get into the play-by-play. For now, stick to the overall game plan. How in the world are you going to do what you said you want to do?

WHY ARE WE DOING THIS?

Why does this change and action even matter? Why is it worth doing all this work? What difference will it make?

WIN → HOW DO WE MEASURE SUCCESS?

How will you know if you're winning? Whenever you play a sport, the scoreboard clearly tells you who is winning. The points are clear, and you can't argue with those. What metrics will show you if you're moving in the right direction?

You may find answers initially to these questions, but don't think that it's a one-and-done process. Along the way, you may need to revisit and refine your answers to be sound in your rationale. Has the problem you're trying to solve changed because of new information? Are there new success criteria? Remember humility. Be willing to take the risk and ask, "Does this still fit, or do we need to realign?" Be ruthless in digging deep to find bedrock and build confidently from there.

Agnes M. Geisler, HRMP, is the Executive Director of People and Processes at Mosaic Christian Church, a non-denominational Christian church located outside Baltimore, Maryland. Agnes has over ten years of experience leading and developing volunteers across multiple campus locations simultaneously, managing change through employee and organizational transitions, site relocations, and expansions, and bringing clarity and clear processes to various aspects of church ministry. From the guest experience to key ministry areas, from operations to HR to college interns, she's affectionately known as a "walking database" who can remember names, faces, and stories for years, because at the end of the day, it's people that matter. Systems and spreadsheets are her bread and butter because they help us ensure we don't miss essential things, whether day-to-day or in the big picture. Our work is too important not to have a system to do it well.

Agnes' prior experience in retail and food service management, training, development, and corporate recruiting has allowed her to thrive in fast-paced, ever-changing environments and lead both volunteers and employees to achieve results and help people never forget their ultimate why in what they're doing.

From experience in a variety of industries, Agnes realized there's a sweet spot in leveraging your skill sets with your passion and values, and found that sweet spot at Mosaic. As a church for people who don't go to church, Mosaic is a place where grace and truth are lived out with radical vulnerability.

Agnes and her college sweetheart Matt have two kids, Elizabeth and Henry. They love cheering on the Baltimore Orioles together, hoping one day they'll celebrate a World Series win back in Charm City. LEGO, puzzles, and volunteering with her kids' soccer teams and a faith-based soul-work organization occupy Agnes' free time and open calendar space.

Connect with Agnes:

Facebook: https://www.facebook.com/agnesmgeisler

Instagram: https://www.instagram.com/agnesmgeisler

LinkedIn: https://www.linkedin.com/in/amgeisler

Learn More about Mosaic: https://mosaicchristian.org

CHAPTER 7

DELIVERING TOUGH NEWS COMPASSIONATELY

FRAN'S FOUR C FRAMEWORK

Sanita Pinchback, MHR, SPHR, SCP

MY STORY

My palms started to sweat. I felt my deodorant fail. *My. Life. Is. Ruined. What am I going to tell everyone? How am I going to find a job? What do I do now? Is there any hope?*

I remember like it was yesterday, those feelings after the recruiter told me, "I wouldn't even bother to apply." It was my dream program—the University of South Carolina's (USC) Master's in International Business (MIB). My heart dropped.

Fast forward 20 years, and I'm sitting in a meeting with all the senior leaders of our plant. Gloria*, our plant leader, said in a sad but firm voice, "After a long process, the decision is final, the company is closing our plant and transferring the work to another location." I knew in my bones our employees needed our leadership. Fran's Four C Framework, which I learned at USC, was just the tool for communicating this type of tough news.

"Announce the closure as soon as possible," I encouraged Gloria. This transparency would allow everyone impacted to prepare for the bumpy road ahead.

We knew from watching the actions of a similar plant that it was critical to develop a solid plan and execute as a team. Our sister plant rushed communications, and the communications were poor and untimely. This lack of transparency broke the trust of the employees. This plant saw employee engagement drop, voluntary attrition rise, and productivity decrease. These metrics were early indicators of trouble. Ultimately, the plant's final production and profits missed expectations by a significant amount.

After several planning sessions, as a plant leadership team, we gathered the employees. The employees felt the gravity of the situation, as we rarely met with all the plant leaders together. Gloria spoke in a strong, calm voice. "We will close the plant in waves. HR will review your severance benefits with you 90 days before your exit date. To the extent we can, we will allow you to stay with the company for as long as possible."

Gloria's voice cracked with emotion as she continued, "We don't know everything, but we will meet with you every two weeks with an update, even if it's to say, 'no update.' We are a team, and we are here to support you."

While listening to Gloria speak, employees displayed a range of emotions. I saw Tracy's eyes widen with shock. She was a 20-year maintenance technician. Herman, a 30-year front-line employee, had his mouth drop open as he processed the news. Karen, our receptionist of 12 years, began to cry softly on her team leader LeAnn's shoulder. The employees started to panic about the changes to come. They looked to the plant leadership team, including me, for guidance.

I was *the* HR leader tasked with delivering the tough news. I knew that the plant closure announcement would cause many employees to experience the "doom spiral." The "doom spiral" is the name I give to the set of emotions I experienced when my dream program, USC's Master's in International Business, told me not to bother applying during the graduate admissions interview so many years ago.

After completing the soul-crushing graduate school admission interview, I ran into Amanda, the career counselor at my undergraduate school, Furman University. Amanda grabbed my hand and took me into her office. She closed the door and gave me a warm, comforting hug. I sobbed for at least five minutes. Not the dainty crying that you see in movies, I'm talking about the ugly cry—me barely able to catch my breath. When my tears slowed to a trickle, my eyes were red, sore, and puffy. My head felt like a mariachi band was playing inside.

She said, "Sanita, what happened?"

In between hiccups and blowing my nose, I described my interaction with USC's recruiter. I explained that with a bored tone and squinted eyes, the recruiter stated, "Sanita, you aren't smart enough to get into USC's MIB program. I wouldn't even bother to apply."

"The recruiter's voice sounded like a staticky radio station afterward," I told Amanda. "I tried to pick up the signal, but it faded." But, as the signal started coming in more clearly, I heard the recruiter mention in a dull voice, "We have this lesser-known Master's in Human Resources program. Because not many people know about the program, it isn't as competitive, so maybe you can get into it."

While I summarized my conversation with USC's recruiter, Amanda began to type on her computer. *Great, I can't even keep her attention.*

Once she finished typing, Amanda showed me her computer screen. With a smile in her voice, she said, "Sanita, USC's Master's in HR program is better suited to your goals." She explained why in detail, and then, she said with confidence, "Regardless of USC's decision on your admission, there are other HR programs and paths available to you. Having the information about your competitiveness for the MIB program gives you more time to choose your path. You can do this."

Amanda's kindness helped me reframe the situation.

In what seemed like a dark moment, she showed me how to leverage the early information to my advantage. I used this time to investigate alternative programs that illuminated my path. This light gave me the confidence to decide how I wanted to move forward. From that moment, I committed to always sharing hard news with compassion. I planned to use Amanda's example of reframing the situation and providing light and hope by suggesting alternate paths.

USC accepted me into their Master's in HR program, and I excelled. As part of our final class, Fran Young, a former Chief Human Resources Officer, provided a framework that clarified Amanda's approach at Furman. I still remember Professor Fran looking over her reading glasses saying, "Being an HR Leader is rewarding, and we must occasionally deliver tough news. These communications are part of our leadership role. At these difficult moments, people will remember most how you made them feel." I remembered the difference Amanda's kindness provided me on that cold November day and how she helped me chart a new path for myself. I never forgot Fran's advice and framework.

Fran's Four C Framework

1. **Communicate Early**—share the bad news as soon as you can.

2. **Compassionately Reframe** the change as an opportunity.

3. **Celebrate Wins**—Share wins to help others think of different options.

4. **Circle Back** to those who are disappointed with their next steps to validate their feelings.

COMMUNICATE EARLY

As time passed from that initial meeting with our employees, the plant updates became a way for us to replace rumors with facts and address fears.

Mario asked, "Is it true that we are going to close the plant early, and everyone will be notified next month?"

I responded, "We're keeping to our originally planned timeline. Our customers still need our products, and the other plant isn't ready to handle the volume."

Karen said, "I don't have a resume, and my computer skills are rusty. How am I going to be able to apply for a job?"

Tracy quickly added to Karen's statement, "I haven't interviewed for a job in over 15 years, I'm nervous I won't measure up."

I explained, "We want you to land on your feet as quickly as possible. My team will provide workshops and interview role-playing sessions for everyone. We will support you. These activities are voluntary, but the company will pay you your regular rate to participate in them."

Consistent, transparent communication built trust with the employees. If we didn't have the answer to their questions, we were honest and said we would get back to them when there was more to share, and we followed through.

COMPASSIONATELY REFRAME

As the first 90-day clock started ticking, we implemented our plan to reframe the news for our employees. We held workshops and hosted practice interview sessions.

During these gatherings, some of our feedback to our employees included:

"Tracy, you nailed that interview question. You provided a great example of how you worked through a challenging process with a co-worker."

"Karen, I didn't know you organized a soccer league for over 100 high school students outside of work. You should definitely include that information in your resume to highlight your leadership experience and decision-making skills."

The feedback we provided our employees gave them the confidence to feel prepared to interview.

To focus our employees on charting a new path, we hosted job fairs with other local employers to help them quickly land new roles.

CELEBRATE WINS

We also asked questions to tap into our employees' imagination. We received some unexpected answers:

- Mario said, "I always wanted to be a nurse, but I had to start working to help provide for my younger siblings. Maybe I will go back to school."
- Tracy, "I've always wanted to be a homeowner. Since I've already landed a new job, I can use my severance money as a down payment on that new home for my family."
- Herman said wistfully, "If I had more free time, I would spend that time with my grandchildren. I worked so much while my kids were young, I feel like I missed out on some key moments."
- LeAnn whispered, "I think I can use the severance to pay off my home early. Having our house paid off would allow me to take a less demanding job and spend more time turning my crafting hobby into a business."

With our employees' permission, we began sharing these exciting ideas for next steps. To our surprise, employees formed support teams of people with similar goals. As employees reached milestones on their new paths, we shared their results and celebrated their accomplishments.

We also celebrated each transition day as a "graduation" to the employees' next chapters. On exit days, the company hosted a big catered lunch to send off each group of impacted employees with style. What was difficult news turned into our employees creating new routes for their lives. They were able to revisit dreams deferred and accelerate other plans. We had employees going back to school, adopting children, paying off their homes early, purchasing their first home, and retiring early to spend more time with their grandchildren.

CIRCLE BACK

As with many changes, we had some employees who were not excited about their next chapter. We set up open "office hours" where employees could come in and have a private conversation with us to share their frustrations with their current situation and their fears about the future. We listened to their concerns and sometimes were able to provide additional avenues or suggestions.

Since not everyone is comfortable asking for help, we also requested team leaders and the line employees who were informal leaders to let us know if they saw someone disengaging or actively struggling with the change. We invited the identified employees in for coffee and a chat. These discussions let the employees know they weren't alone.

Change is difficult, and not everyone adapts well. For these employees, we confirmed we saw their continued struggle with the changes and assured them we would help in any way we could.

RESULTS

There was a lot of pride at this plant. The work our employees performed improved lives and kept thousands of tons of waste out of landfills every year. As a plant leadership team, we tapped into this pride and set a united goal of finishing our time at this plant strongly. "Finish Strong" became our rallying cry.

Even though the plant was closing, our efforts led to improved employee morale. Because we were transparent about our plans to close the plant, complaints about favoritism dropped significantly. We asked for input on how we could change our manufacturing processes as we ramped down.

Implementing these changes increased plant productivity. Employees felt seen, heard, and valued, so we also saw voluntary attrition decline. The increased engagement, improved productivity, and decrease in voluntary attrition allowed us to Finish Strong by delivering our commitments on production and profitability.

One of the company's senior regional leaders visited our plant and said with awe in his voice, "I just came from a plant where we're investing millions of dollars, but those employees were not nearly as engaged as this team, for whom we're closing their plant in a few months. Sanita, *what* are you doing differently here?"

We told him our simple formula:

1. **Communicate Early**
2. **Compassionately Reframe**
3. **Celebrate Wins**
4. **Circle Back**

If you had told me, when my spirits were crushed, that I would one day be grateful that USC's recruiter told me not to bother applying for the MIB program, I wouldn't have believed you. However, thanks to that experience, I've consistently worked to deliver tough news with a sense of hope.

* Note – All names have been changed to protect the innocent.

THE TOOL

As I write this chapter, with over 25 years of living between me and that cold November day, I realize we all deliver difficult news at some point in our lives. Whether it is a budget cut, program cancellation, or a layoff, these communications may change people's lives. I'd like to share with you Fran's Four Cs so you can reframe the situation to give the people you care about the confidence to chart their next chapter.

FRAN'S FOUR C FRAMEWORK

1. **Communicate Early** to build trust. This notification provides time to develop alternative paths. Bad news is like fish; the longer you hold it, the worse it smells.

   - Share as much as you can as soon as possible.
   - Welcome and encourage questions.
   - Give people an opportunity to work through their disappointment about what could have been so that they can chart a new course.
   - Provide regular updates to keep the lines of communication open.

2. **Compassionately Reframe** the change and offer alternative lanes. Reframing the change interrupts the "doom spiral" thoughts. Ask a question to refocus energy into finding a new way forward.

   - Provide perspective on how they can use knowledge, skills, and experiences from hobbies or volunteer work to chart a new work path.
   - Point out resources to build new skills.
   - Encourage them to tap into dreams deferred by asking them to recall a time when they wanted to do something special.

3. **Celebrate Wins** to expand points of view.

   - Share examples of how others used the information to create a new direction for their lives, which may spark an interest in the possible.
   - Connect people with similar interests together so they can encourage each other.
   - Identify and celebrate milestones as you move toward the "new normal" to build positive anticipation.

4. **Circle Back** to everyone, because change is hard.

   - There is no situation where everyone will be happy with the change. However, it is important that everyone's feelings are validated.

- Encourage people to express disappointment, which may help them process their emotions and continue to move through the change instead of becoming stuck.

- Provide a compassionate ear for those who struggle with the change or were disappointed in their next steps. Confirm you see them and will help in any way you can.

If you are preparing to deliver news that will challenge someone's identity, future, or livelihood, we can work through it together to create your plan. Contact me at sanita@pinchbackadvisory.com.

FOR BONUS CONTENT

Click https://www.pinchbackadvisory.com/download for a downloadable copy of questions that can help you reframe a change and Fran's Four C Framework.

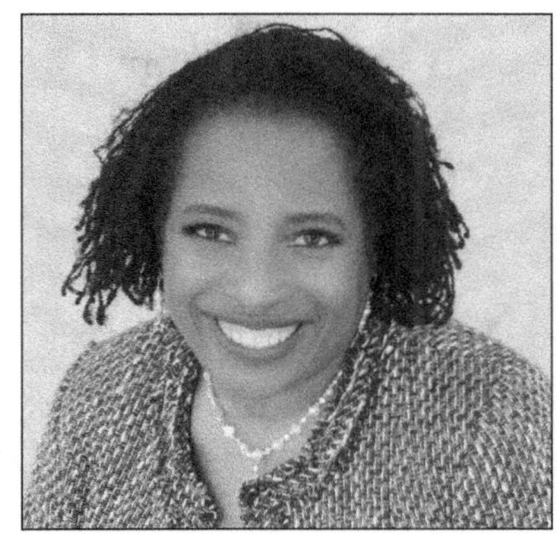

Sanita Pinchback, MHR, SPHR, and SCP, is the Founder and CEO of Pinch Back Advisory, which specializes in guiding emerging consumer package goods (CPG) businesses to grow through intentional focus. Sanita is an innovative and strategic HR leader with more than 25 years of demonstrated excellence. She has created simple HR practices that deliver high-value impact and goal-focused outcomes to businesses of all sizes. Her breadth of experience runs from Fortune 500 companies to entrepreneurial start-ups in multiple industries including, consumer package goods, distribution, and medical devices.

Sanita's mission is to help leaders develop the clarity and confidence to tell the world their story in their own voice. She does this by understanding the leader's vision for their business and translating it into actionable steps for their team. She's found that when the team knows the direction and expectations, they make smarter decisions that fuel growth. This improved decision-making frees the leader to dream of the next big hill to conquer.

Sanita and her husband, Scott, live in the Dallas, Texas, metroplex. When Sanita isn't fueling other people's dreams, she loves to explore new places. She's lived in six of the 50 United States and is closing in on visiting all 50. She has five states in the heart of the lower 48 to tackle! When she needs to recharge, Sanita can be found in a hammock by the beach sipping a cold beverage, listening to jazz, and reading a happily-ever-after book (because life is tough enough).

Connect with Sanita:

Website: https://www.pinchbackadvisory.com/

Email: sanita@pinchbackadvisory.com

PART II

WHY PEOPLE STAY— OR LEAVE

HOW SUCCESS IS REALLY BUILT

CHAPTER 8

WHY HR SHOULD CARE ABOUT RELATIONSHIP CAPITAL

HOW TRUST DRIVES CULTURE AND RESULTS

Jill A. Rogers, ACC, PMP

"Relationship capital is what people give you the benefit of when it matters most."

- Jill A. Rogers

MY STORY

THE ANNOUNCEMENT

"On a personal note, I need to let you know I have breast cancer." I took a deep breath, readying myself to launch into the bullet points I rehearsed about my upcoming leave of absence.

I have to be prepared for all of their questions, I thought. *Emphasize "risk mitigation" and "ensuring continuity of operations."*

The last five minutes of each weekly client status meeting are spent going around the table to discuss anything not yet covered. "Oh, there is one more thing," I choked out as the now-familiar tingle in the backs of my eyes indicated tears were on their way again. I was well-prepared with my talking points, but never had to use them. Instead, I just listened.

"Oh, Jill, we've got you while you've got this. Let us take it from here while you take the time you need for yourself and your family." That quickly became a familiar refrain from my clients, employees, teaming partners, consultants, vendors, and countless others.

As the founder of a small consulting company, I'm quite familiar with working behind the scenes and rolling up my sleeves to accomplish our clients' goals. One of my mantras—and the foundation of our approach to client services—is "We work for you. Your success is our success. Period." This is a space I was most comfortable in.

This feeling of being taken care of, of relying on others' goodwill and insistence to let them help, was an unfamiliar one, to say the least. But it also felt like putting on a clean sweatshirt fresh from the dryer. It was warm and comforting at a time when I felt very vulnerable and unsure about my future and my business's future.

In 18 years of building my company, I quickly discovered I also built up a significant amount of relationship capital, even though I didn't realize it had a name until two years ago. My cancer diagnosis prompted the "redeeming" of my relationship capital. It's what people "give you the benefit of" when it matters most. In my case, it was the initiative, showing up, and taking care of what needed to be done for me, my family, and my company when I could not. This experience of being taken care of by my colleagues, employees, and partners while I was truly "unavailable," not only enhanced my understanding of how I do business but taught me first-hand about the critical role of relationship capital as a business asset.

Since then, I learned that relationship capital is more than strong relationships and trust; it is actually a scalable business asset. One that can be taught, operationalized, measured, and found in thriving organizational cultures. One that impacts productivity, efficiency, turnover, collaboration, and engagement.

THE EPIPHANY

How did I get from experiencing first-hand supportive personal and professional networks to operationalizing relationship capital as a business strategy? It started about three years ago by writing a book, of course!

The intent of my book, *It's Not Just Who You Know*, was to share my lessons learned and insights into the somewhat complex world of small-business government contracting, gleaned from more than 25 years in this space. I hoped to accelerate the learning curve, which can be steep, for those considering entry into this market, all while fulfilling my long-time personal goal of becoming a published author. In the back of my mind, I was also looking for a transition from managing the business to coaching, mentoring, and guiding other small business owners as they launch theirs.

When I turned 50 a few years ago, I embraced the milestone and decided it was time to write my book. I never felt better. I was truly comfortable in my own skin, with a deep understanding of my strengths, weaknesses, and value. I raised three young men who bring me tremendous joy, give me purpose, and made me a hockey mom. I exercised regularly and felt strong, able to keep up with my boys on black diamonds, long days at the rink, and an occasional turkey trot.

I engaged with a company that helps first-time authors like me. I followed their process steps to develop my topic, define my ideal reader profile, create chapter themes and supporting stories of my experiences for each, and boom, I was on my way!

I didn't get very far. Three months into weekly meetings with my writing support team, countless hours of self-reflection on my 25 years in this industry, and narrowing down the experiences I wanted to share in the book, I received notice of an irregular mammogram and a request for additional imaging.

I wasn't worried. *I feel great. I have a decade of annual mammograms that have never presented any abnormalities, until now.*

I truly felt I hit my stride at age 50, so two weeks after turning 51, hearing the words "you have cancer" didn't seem possible. Finding out my best course of treatment was a double mastectomy, also not possible. Four to six weeks of recovery post-op, *are you kidding me? I'm a small business owner. I'm always available to be reached. How is this going to work?*

And then, in the quiet of my mind, just like after the power goes out during a storm, that familiar hummmm sound of my internal generator named "resilience" kicked in.

The weeks immediately after my diagnosis were a blur filled with appointments for additional testing and imaging, consults with a variety of health care providers and physicians, and my own research and data gathering. "What questions should I be asking you that I haven't already?" is my favorite go-to when meeting new client organizations. It served me well for years in consulting, and turns out, it is pretty effective with each new medical consult. *This is good, I can approach it this way.*

"I'd like to make an appointment to see the Doctor" became a familiar refrain.

"Yes, I am an active cancer patient." *What a strange question*, but that question became a common one used to prioritize my appointment over other new patients. The "customer service" girl in me appreciated that approach and made me feel right at home.

I was very much in consultant vs. patient mode, treating my diagnosis as a new project to solve with a whole new set of stakeholders. This was my comfort zone. This was how I could handle what seemed impossible. Utilizing my data collection skills to inform decisions for my health care was familiar, empowering, and comforting.

I quickly moved from "this is not possible" to this is reality. It was easy to make subsequent decisions and move forward quickly when I put my children and my health first, above everything. Fighting cancer was the only project on my list now. The book was on hold indefinitely, and that was an easy decision.

COMING FULL CIRCLE

"Cancer-free." Hearing those words, seeing them in print, now makes the backs of my eyes tingle, but the tears don't fall anymore. An overwhelming sense of gratitude is the feeling behind the tingle now. Grateful for my family, my medical team, my personal village, and work family, I looked forward to the healthy road ahead. Did it include getting back to finishing my book? I wasn't sure, and I was okay with that.

One year later, I did finish the book. It provided an invaluable creative outlet and an epiphany during my recovery. Turns out, I was writing a book focused on relationship capital the entire time, I just didn't realize it. I never heard that term before, let alone considered it the theme of my book. But looking back on my 28-month writing timeline, which included stops and starts, this was the overarching concept from the beginning.

This journey started with a personal goal to write a book, but became a story about the value of relationships. During the initial phases of planning the outline, my brain was on overdrive with excitement, churning through 25 years of reflection and a strong desire to provide value. *I hope I'm picking the best, most helpful, and most valuable lessons I have for my ideal reader.*

At some point in this book-writing journey, I realized that my ideal reader isn't just someone trying to gain additional perspective on the workings of the government contracting space to build a sustainable business. This book is for anyone curious about relationship capital, what it means, how it develops over time, and the impact of that return on investment every day, especially in a crisis when you need it most.

I set out to share my own lessons learned, and, in fact, the tables turned. I realized that what truly matters when building a sustainable business is the people—employees, clients, teaming partners, colleagues, and other service providers—who enable continuity of operations because they're invested. This is my definition of relationship capital.

While I will not go so far as to say I'm glad I had cancer, the perspective I gleaned from this book shaped me in a way I never expected and is a gift, as they say, that keeps on giving.

PAYING IT FORWARD

I'm grateful for the opportunity to contribute to this book and share a very personal example of the impact of relationship capital on my business. I believe that genuine relationships drive long-term success because I've experienced it first-hand. Whether it's knowing your customer or treating employees and partners with intention, organizations thrive by listening first, staying consistent, and connecting with intention. Every customer, partner, and team member is treated as a long-term relationship, not a short-term transaction.

"Customers may forget what you said, but they will never forget how you made them feel." Horst Schulze, former president and cofounder of The Ritz-Carlton Hotel Company.

My journey to discovering the impact of relationship capital started 30 years ago when I was hired at The Ritz-Carlton, Buckhead, fresh out of undergrad. I was introduced to a concept that changed my perspective and has stayed with me for life, both consciously and unconsciously. I started in orientation, like all new employees, where I first heard "We are ladies and gentlemen serving ladies and gentlemen." Then there was more (a credo) which we were asked to memorize. It talked about the hotel being a place where the genuine care of our guests was our highest mission. It went on about how we strive to provide them with the highest quality personal service, etc. It ends with a statement about fulfilling guests' wants and needs—even those they didn't express—by anticipating them. We were even given a trifold laminated card with the credo to carry in our pockets.

I quickly learned those were not just words, and their meaning did not end when I left orientation. Over the next three years, I learned first-hand what an operationalized corporate culture built on clearly defined values looked like, acted like, and, more importantly, felt like. They formed the building blocks of my philosophy of customer service, the lifetime value of a guest (or client), and how to sell an experience.

The Ritz-Carlton's values also contained direct and indirect linkages to employee satisfaction, customer retention, and profit. Not only were these good ideas, but they also impacted the bottom line, making them sound business practices. It started to click for me; *relationships are the infrastructure of performance.*

This concept applies to all industries—not only hospitality or professional services—since every organization is built on relationships. In my company, this means warm introductions over cold outreach, honest communication over pressure, and steady follow-up over quick wins. By building trust at every step, we increase referrals, strengthen loyalty, and create a network that supports sustainable growth.

The relationship capital assessment brings these ideas together into a practical framework that business owners, HR leaders, and others can assess and influence directly. The following section suggests an assessment as a first step to explore the current strength of relationship capital in organizations.

THE TOOL

THE JRC RELATIONSHIP CAPITAL ASSESSMENT

As described in my book, *It's Not Just Who You Know*, sustainable business advantage is created not through visibility alone, but through intentional, trust-based relationships built over time. My book demonstrates that relationship capital compounds when credibility, consistency, and reciprocity are treated as strategic assets rather than soft skills.

Any business, regardless of industry, can operationalize these principles by embedding relationship-building into core growth, sales, and partnership processes. This assessment measures how trust, communication, and relationships are working across the organization. Where relationship capital is strong, performance accelerates. Where it's weak, everything costs more.

IS YOUR ORGANIZATION SET UP TO MAXIMIZE ITS RELATIONSHIP ROI?

The JRC Relationship Capital assessment is a starting point for anyone—business owners, company culture leaders, HR professionals—as a high-level diagnostic to understand which areas are working well and where opportunities for improvement exist. It can serve as a launching point to explore ways to increase relationship capital in your organization through a variety of approaches.

When positioned as a scalable business asset, relationship capital impacts every department from HR to finance to sales. It's the sum of how much people trust you or your company, how willing they are to help you (or buy a product from you), how well you communicate, and how strong your reputation is over time (quality). Unlike financial or intellectual capital, relationship capital is built through consistent behavior, not transactions.

It grows when people feel respected, heard, and confident that promises will be kept.

To determine the baseline of your organization's relationship capital index, assess the following 30 statements using a 5-point scale, honestly, based on day-to-day reality, not intent. This diagnostic can be used annually to determine the impact of any relationship capital improvement initiatives over time.

INSTRUCTIONS

Rate each statement on a scale of 1–5:

1 = Strongly disagree

2 = Disagree

3 = Neutral

4 = Agree

5 = Strongly agree

SECTION 1: TRUST & CREDIBILITY

Rating (1-5)

1. Employees trust leadership to follow through on commitments.

2. Leaders communicate clearly and consistently.

3. Decisions are explained, not just announced.

4. People feel safe raising concerns without fear of retaliation.

5. Mistakes are handled fairly and constructively.

SECTION 2: MANAGER-EMPLOYEE RELATIONSHIPS — Rating (1-5)

6. Managers regularly check in beyond task updates. ________

7. Employees feel seen and valued by their manager. ________

8. Feedback is timely, specific, and respectful. ________

9. Expectations are clear and reinforced consistently. ________

10. Managers model the behavior they expect from others. ________

SECTION 3: COLLABORATION & PEER RELATIONSHIPS — Rating (1-5)

11. Teams collaborate across departments effectively. ________

12. Information is shared freely, not hoarded. ________

13. Conflicts are addressed directly and respectfully. ________

14. People are willing to help each other without being asked. ________

15. Informal influencers positively shape team culture. ________

SECTION 4: COMMUNICATION & FOLLOW-THROUGH — Rating (1-5)

16. Important messages are communicated clearly and repeatedly. ________

17. Follow-up is consistent and reliable. ________

18. Employees know where to go for answers. ________

19. Meetings lead to action, not confusion. ________

20. Communication builds clarity rather than tension. ________

SECTION 5: CULTURE & BELONGING — Rating (1-5)

21. Employees feel a sense of belonging. ________

22. Values are reflected in daily behavior, not just words. ________

23. Recognition feels genuine and timely. ________

24. New employees are integrated quickly and intentionally. ________

25. People feel proud to be part of the organization. ________

SECTION 6: CHANGE & RESILIENCE   Rating (1-5)

26. Leaders communicate early during change.   __________

27. Employees understand the "why" behind change.   __________

28. Trust is maintained during periods of uncertainty.   __________

29. Teams adapt quickly without breakdowns in morale.   __________

30. Relationships remain strong under pressure.   __________

SCORING THE ASSESSMENT—TOTAL POSSIBLE SCORE: 150

- **120–150 (Strong Relationship Capital)** Trust is high. Communication is effective. The organization is resilient and collaborative.

- **90–119 (Moderate Relationship Capital)** Relationships are functional but inconsistent. Risk of disengagement or breakdown under stress.

- **Below 90 (Weak Relationship Capital)**, trust gaps exist. Communication and follow-through are likely hurting retention, performance, or morale.

WHY SHOULD HR LEADERS CARE ABOUT RELATIONSHIP CAPITAL?

HR is in a unique position to affect the strength and presence of relationship capital in an organization. As the center of an organization's relationship ecosystem, HR doesn't just manage people; it shapes how people relate to each other, to leaders, and to the company itself. Understanding how trust drives culture and results is the first step in building an organization with high relationship capital.

Jill A. Rogers, ACC, PMP, is the CEO of JRogers Consulting LLC (JRC). With more than 25 years in federal government consulting, her passion for customer service remains at the center of her job description and JRC's core values. She enjoys rolling up her sleeves and getting into the details with her teams. She thrives on helping organizations improve their effectiveness by designing and delivering customized solutions that meet their needs and exceed expectations.

Ms. Rogers' high standards for customer service, the basis for JRC's philosophy on client service, were developed early in her career during her tenure at The Ritz-Carlton Hotel Company. Her consulting skills were cultivated in the "big firm" environments of PricewaterhouseCoopers, IBM Business Consulting, and Booz Allen Hamilton.

She founded JRC in 2006 to continue her passion for client service while balancing life changes. By 2012, JRC had grown exponentially in size, the number of contracts, and the breadth and depth of its capabilities. Often asked how her business grew organically so quickly, Ms. Rogers says, "We don't try to be all things to all people. We do what we do very well and with the highest levels of quality and professionalism. We work for our clients and partners to make them look good. Period."

Ms. Rogers has a Bachelor of Arts in Political Science from The Catholic University of America and earned her Executive Coaching Certificate through Philosophy IB/American University. She is an Associate Certified Coach (ACC) with the International Coaching Federation (ICF), a Project Management Professional (PMP), a Certified Professional Culture Facilitator (CPCF), and certified to administer a variety of leadership assessments. She is a member of the Women for Change Coaching Community and a hockey mom of three young men committed to learning something new every day.

Connect with Jill:

Website: https://www.jrcllc.com

LinkedIn: https://www.linkedin.com/in/jill-rogers-acc-pmp-b25a60/

Facebook: https://www.facebook.com/profile.php?id=100064177264109

CHAPTER 9

BEYOND THE PAYCHECK

HOW MONEY WORKS FOR EMPLOYEES AND BUSINESS OWNERS

Adina M. Lavoie, RVP, IAR

MY STORY

"I'm sorry we couldn't afford to get you a nice watch."

That's the part I remember most.

December 1992. I walked across the stage at my college graduation with only my mom in the audience to witness it. My dad was overseas, on an unaccompanied tour with the United States Navy. My sister was working through college and was too busy with her boyfriend to make the trip from Annapolis, Maryland, to Durham, New Hampshire.

I can't remember where we went to eat after it was over. But I will never forget my mom saying those words. She made it very clear how proud she—and Dad—were of me for graduating from college. And yet, to her, the fact that she couldn't keep her word on a promise of such a generous gift gutted her.

To my mom, the watch wasn't about time; it was about proof—proof that the long hours, the stretched budgets, the sacrifices that never came with fanfare, added up to something tangible. A watch marked achievement. It said: *You made it.* And in her mind, not being able to give me that symbol felt like falling short—even though everything else she and my dad did made that moment possible in the first place.

She always believed in planning for what mattered—in envelopes, in careful choices, in doing the best you could with what you had and never pretending money didn't matter—because when it was tight, it mattered even more. What I didn't realize then was that the apology wasn't really about a watch at all. It was about a system of values she lived by, quietly and consistently, long before I understood how much it would shape the way I see work, money, and success.

For years, I witnessed my dad take extra weekend duty, study for promotions, shine his boots to a pristine condition, and always step up when asked. He was in the Navy for almost 30 years. He retired in his early 50s, but his pension wasn't enough to support them without work. So, off he went looking for something to keep him busy, and he took a job at the United States Naval Academy (USNA), working to support the midshipmen in logistics.

My mom always worked, sometimes 50-60 hours a week, as a civilian with the Navy, in HR at the Naval Academy. They were up early and home late most days, but like many, had the weekends off. As kids, we packed a picnic and went into Washington, D.C., on Sunday afternoons after church to visit a museum, walk through the Torpedo Factory in Alexandria, or visit the National Arboretum and eat roast beef sandwiches with mustard under the shade of the trees. If you asked me about those Sundays when I was a child, I think I would've told you I hated them; now, what I wouldn't give to have them back.

THE ENVELOPE SYSTEM

As a kid, maybe 10 or 12 years old, I remember going to the bank on Saturday mornings with my mom and sister. Mom cashed their paychecks and got the money (actual cash) back in a little bank envelope with two lollipops, one for me and one for my sister, Christine. At home, she sat at the kitchen table writing out the bills for the week, separating the money into little piles, and putting it in envelopes marked "Electric," "Rent," or "Groceries." She did this every week for as long as I can remember. I don't recall ever being hungry, not having two dollars for the church collection, or ever going without presents under the Christmas tree. But I never did get that Rolex.

In 2007, my sister called me one day and said, "Have you talked to Mom?" I said, "No, why?" She said, "I'm pregnant!" What a thrill to hear I would be an aunt again; I was so excited. The cold of January came, and so did a little blond-haired baby boy named Mitchell. We brought him straight home to Annapolis to show Mom and Dad. I'll never forget placing him in Mom's arms and her saying, "I can't feel him, please take him back. I don't want to drop him." Our lives changed in an instant. We didn't know what to think, but we knew that something was very wrong with our mom.

The following week, my mom was taken to Bethesda National Medical Center. She was misdiagnosed with Leukemia, Lou Gehrig's Disease, Guillain-Barré syndrome, and congestive heart failure. None of them was correct. None of the President's doctors knew what was wrong with her. It was the longest eight months of my life. She never recovered.

A few days later, we had an appointment with the funeral home to make her arrangements. Before we left the house, my dad said to me, "Do you know where Mom keeps the checkbook?" I walked into her room and pulled it from her little side table by the recliner. My mom still wrote the bills out by hand every Saturday morning. My dad didn't know when he got paid. He didn't know he had an American Express card. He didn't know when the electric bill was due.

Gay, my mom's coworker, called several weeks after she passed away. "Have you sent in all the paperwork for your mom's death benefits?" she wanted to know. All I can say is, thank God my mom was in HR. She knew all the boxes to check and the choices to make for her family to be taken care of in the event of her untimely death. That day was the first time I saw my dad cry. That was the day I knew I was being called to help people better understand how money works.

I have a college degree in Business, Finance, and Marketing. I could run multi-million-dollar businesses, but didn't know the first thing about life insurance, 401(k)s, personal budgets, retirement, or Social Security. I watched my mom and dad survive paycheck to paycheck for their entire lives. I started to imagine a business where I could help people with some of the most important decisions of their lives. I wanted to help people like my dad, sister, and me become better educated about making good financial decisions. I wanted to help my dad retire with some dignity. Thanks to my mom, I did just that.

My story is precisely why I want to share with you next how financial literacy can empower everyone in your organization.

WHY FINANCIAL LITERACY EMPOWERS EMPLOYEES AND SMALL BUSINESS OWNERS

Money affects almost every part of our daily lives. Whether someone is earning a salary or running a small business, financial decisions play a big role in determining stability, success, and peace of mind. Financial literacy simply means having the knowledge and skills to understand money, how to earn it, manage it, save it, borrow it, and plan for the future.

For employees, financial literacy helps them stretch their income, avoid or misuse debt, and prepare for long-term goals like education for children, a first-time home purchase, and retirement. For small business owners, it helps them manage cash, make smart business decisions, avoid financial mistakes, and grow their businesses. In both cases, financial literacy gives people more control over their lives, reduces uncertainty and stress, and promotes financial decisions based on logic rather than emotions.

WHAT IS FINANCIAL LITERACY?

Financial literacy is the ability to understand and use basic money concepts. These include budgeting, saving, investing, borrowing, insurance, and planning for the future. It's not about becoming a financial expert. Instead, it's about knowing enough to make smart, informed choices about money.

A financially literate person can answer simple but important questions, such as:

- How much money do I earn and spend each month?
- How can I save for emergencies?
- Is this loan affordable?
- What happens if I do not plan?

For employees and small business owners, answering these questions helps them avoid money troubles and build a more secure future.

HOW FINANCIAL LITERACY EMPOWERS EMPLOYEES

Better Control of Personal Finances

One of the biggest benefits of financial literacy for employees is learning how to manage their money better. When employees understand how to budget, they can plan how to use their income wisely. This helps ensure that basic needs like rent, food, and transportation are covered while still leaving room for savings.

Financially literate employees can:

- Track how much they earn and spend
- Save money regularly
- Prepare for emergencies

- Avoid overspending
- Set financial goals

Having control over personal finances gives employees confidence and reduces the stress that often comes from money problems.

LESS DEBT AND FEWER FINANCIAL CHALLENGES

Many employees struggle with debt—credit cards, personal loans, or student loans. Without financial knowledge, it's easy to borrow too much or misunderstand interest rates and repayment terms. This can lead to ongoing financial trouble.

Financial literacy helps employees understand:

- How interest works
- The true cost of borrowing
- How to compare loan options
- How to pay off debt faster

With this knowledge, employees can make smarter borrowing decisions and avoid falling into debt traps. Less debt means fewer financial emergencies and a more stable financial life.

IMPROVED FOCUS AND PRODUCTIVITY AT WORK

Money stress does not stay at home—it often follows employees to work. Worrying about bills, loans, or emergencies can affect concentration, performance, and motivation. Financially literate employees are better prepared to handle financial challenges, which can lower stress levels.

When employees feel financially secure:

- They're more focused at work
- They take fewer sick days
- They feel more satisfied with their jobs
- They're more productive and engaged

This benefits not only employees but also employers, who gain a more focused, committed workforce.

BETTER PREPARATION FOR RETIREMENT AND THE FUTURE

Many employees do not plan enough for retirement because they don't understand how retirement savings work. Financial literacy helps employees learn about savings plans, pensions, and long-term investing.

Financially literate employees understand:

- The importance of saving early
- How compound interest helps money grow
- How employer retirement plans work
- Why long-term planning matters
- What will social security benefits be in the future

This knowledge empowers employees to prepare for the future and reduce the risk of financial hardship later in life, and this is why I want to share my learning with you.

THE TOOL

EMPOWERING EMPLOYEES AND

Small Business Owners Through Financial Literacy

Based on my own experience and years of working with friends, family, clients, and more, these are my seven key tips for understanding the basics of navigating the money side of your life.

1. Smarter Business Decisions

Running a small business involves making financial decisions every day. These include setting prices, hiring staff, buying supplies, and deciding when to expand. Without financial knowledge, business owners may rely on guesswork, leading to costly mistakes.

Financial literacy helps small business owners:

- Understand basic financial reports
- Keep personal and business assets separate
- Know whether the business is making a profit
- Decide where to invest money
- Plan for the future

This knowledge allows business owners to make decisions based on facts rather than assumptions.

2. Stronger Cash Flow Management

Many small businesses fail not because they lack customers, but because they run out of cash. Cash flow refers to the money coming into and going out of a business. Financial literacy helps business owners understand and manage cash flow properly.

With financial literacy, business owners can:

- Track income and expenses
- Plan for slow seasons
- Pay bills and employees on time
- Set aside money for emergencies

Good cash flow management helps businesses stay open and stable, even during tough times.

3. Better Access to Loans and Funding

Small business owners often need loans or outside funding to grow their businesses. Financial literacy helps them understand loan terms and prepare the documents lenders require.

Financially literate business owners can:

- Create clear business plans
- Understand interest rates and fees
- Choose the right type of loan
- Avoid borrowing more than they can afford

This makes it easier to access funding while reducing the risk of debt problems.

4. Better Cost Control and Higher Profits

Understanding money helps business owners control costs and improve profits. Financial literacy allows them to see where money is being wasted and where improvements can be made.

With financial knowledge, business owners can:

- Cut unnecessary expenses
- Set fair and profitable prices
- Improve efficiency
- Focus on activities that bring the most value

This leads to stronger, more profitable businesses.

5. Long-Term Business Growth and Stability

Financial literacy also supports long-term success. Business owners who understand financial risks can plan growth more carefully and avoid taking unnecessary chances.

They can:

- Decide when expansion makes sense
- Manage debt wisely
- Build savings for difficult periods
- Create stable, lasting businesses

This empowers small business owners to move beyond survival and build businesses that grow and create jobs.

6. Wider Benefits to Society and the Economy

GREATER ECONOMIC STABILITY

When employees and business owners manage money well, the entire economy benefits. Financially stable individuals are less likely to default on loans or need emergency assistance. Strong small businesses help stabilize local economies and communities.

JOB CREATION AND BUSINESS GROWTH

Small businesses are key sources of jobs and innovation. Financially literate entrepreneurs are more likely to succeed, grow, and hire others. This helps strengthen economies and improve living standards.

7. The Importance of Financial Education

Financial literacy does not happen automatically. It must be taught and supported. Schools, employers, governments, and community organizations all play a role in improving financial education.

Employers can help by offering:

- Financial wellness programs
- Retirement planning education
- Access to financial advice

In summary, financial literacy equips employees and small business owners with the tools to take control of their financial lives. For employees, it reduces stress, improves money management, and supports long-term security. For small business owners, it leads to better decisions, stronger cash flow, and sustainable growth.

Beyond individual benefits, financial literacy strengthens economies, creates jobs, and promotes fairness and opportunity. In today's complex financial world, understanding money is not optional; it's essential.

By investing in financial education and promoting financial literacy, individuals gain confidence, businesses become stronger, and communities grow more resilient. Financial literacy is not just about money; it's about empowerment, stability, and a better future for all.

WHAT'S NEXT?

Here are some action steps to establish a budget and understand where all the money goes.

- Gather your most recent pay stubs
- Print your last three months of bank statements for all accounts, including checking, savings, and retirement accounts in IRAs or 401(k), 403b, or 457, and employer-sponsored plans
- Retrieve ALL current statements for any mortgages, credit cards, car loans, and student loans
- Find a basic budget worksheet to identify monthly expenses such as utilities, gas, subscriptions, travel, entertainment, education, and food. This is a great spot to review your credit card statements and categorize the charges and average monthly expenses

Now, take the time to sit down and write it out. I would suggest a legal pad and a pencil, and starting at the top, categorize income and expenses. This simple exercise can be very cathartic and eye-opening. You will identify things like how much you are spending on dining out, coffee, or children's sports and activities. This is just an opportunity to see what categories are "eating up" the dollars coming in every month and how you can begin to take control of where you actually want them to go.

Understand, people don't plan to fail; they fail to plan.

Adina M. Lavoie was born in Manchester, New Hampshire. Growing up in New England meant moose antlers on the walls, summers on the lake, winters on a skidoo, and cheering on the Boston Red Sox and New England Patriots.

Her family moved to Annapolis, Maryland, when her father was relocated for work. Not long after, he re-enlisted in the US Navy, and they moved overseas for several years. When it was time for college, she returned to the States to attend the University of New Hampshire, where she studied business and was closer to her relatives.

After college, her parents had been assigned to the US Naval Academy. She found work in the local restaurant scene, starting a management training program with Pizzeria Uno's. Looking for new opportunities and career development, she worked in franchising for almost 15 years with OSI Brands and Outback Steakhouse.

When her mother fell ill in 2007, she became her patient advocate. She worked closely with doctors during the final months of her life to ensure the best possible care. After her death, she began studies and licensure in the financial services industry to support her dad and help families, much as she had done for her own.

She and her dedicated team help families in and around the entire DMV area. She lives in Annapolis, Maryland, and has called it home for over 30 years. Her cats, Spike and Frankie, keep her busy asking for head rubs and treats. Oh, and Mitchell, the little blond-haired baby boy, is an Eagle Scout preparing to graduate high school and head to St. Anselm College. He wants to be a dentist.

Connect with Adina:

Websites: https://www.primerica.com/public/
www.digifinancial.com
https://www.primerica.com/adinamlavoie

Email: mpjh2@primerica.com

LinkedIn: https://www.linkedin.com/in/adinamlavoiepfs/

CHAPTER 10

HR AS A BUSINESS PARTNER, NOT A DEPARTMENT

BECAUSE PEOPLE DECISIONS ARE BUSINESS DECISIONS

Jaime Damkroger, MBA, PHR

MY STORY

One of my most prized possessions isn't a degree, a certification, or an award. It's a framed knob.

The frame is black, five by seven inches, with a bright yellow mat. Inside the frame is a knob that resembles a Master Lock, surrounded by hand-drawn sketches commemorating my time at a manufacturing facility early in my career. It has traveled with me to every desk, every office, and every role I've held over the past fifteen years.

I keep it because it reminds me not only of how out of place I felt the day I walked onto that manufacturing floor, but, more importantly, how I felt the day I left.

"Wait, that tiny knob controls that entire machine?!" I asked.

Mike, the first-shift press operator, looked at me like I had three eyes.

To be fair, I was wearing safety glasses (along with a hair net, hard hat, and steel-toed boots), and my question was genuine. I was on the floor, shadowing team members, trying to understand how the work actually happened.

When I asked that innocent question, I'm not sure Mike even responded, other than a grunt. He quickly followed it with, "Please don't touch anything," which spoke volumes about the level of trust he had in me.

It was hard for me to believe something so small could have such a major impact. It controlled a printing press that dominated the floor like a small building lying on its side. The press stretched the length of a semi-truck and stood two stories tall, pulling wide rolls of paper through a maze of steel rollers and printing stations.

A significant portion of my HR career was spent at a Consumer Packaged Goods (CPG) company. I worked in the corporate office, where there was a firm belief that if you wanted to advance in HR, you had to spend time in a manufacturing facility. On paper, that made complete sense. In reality, it felt almost impossible.

I had recently gotten married, an exciting time of life that came with a new home, a spouse's career, plans for kids, and putting down roots. Relocating wasn't an option for me. There was a facility about thirty minutes from where I lived, but those roles were highly sought after. Everyone in HR was chasing the same thing: manufacturing experience. And when those seats opened, the competition was tough.

So I got creative.

During a regularly scheduled one-on-one meeting, I broached the topic with my boss. "Would you ever consider a temporary assignment? A short-term way to gain the experience?"

I knew there were facilities across the U.S., and I hoped to avoid uprooting my entire newly established life. In my mind, I pictured filling in while someone was out on maternity leave, a few months, a learning opportunity, a box checked.

I learned the "be careful what you ask for" lesson quickly.

The following week, I was on a plane bound for a newly vacated HR role at a facility in another state. However, this wasn't a temporary backfill. The HR Manager had recently been let go.

I knew I was walking into a challenge. I just didn't yet understand how steep the uphill climb would be.

As I dug in, I learned many members of the leadership team were barely keeping their heads above water themselves. They were trapped between cost-cutting initiatives, production demands, people challenges, and declining engagement. The company had recently run an engagement survey, and the results were brutal; there was no softer word for it.

During my first month at the facility, I sat in my office catching up on work when an employee stopped by with a question. I gave him what I thought was a solid, textbook HR response. He paused, smirked a little, and tossed out an off-the-cuff comment: "How would you know? You're a carpet walker."

I stopped him immediately. "Wait, what was that?"

He looked a bit embarrassed and repeated it more plainly. "You're a carpet walker."

It took a moment to sink in. My office had carpet. The production floor didn't. On the surface, it was pretty funny, and I laughed.

But once the humor wore off, something heavier settled in. *Oh, I get it. I'm not one of them.*

That comment wasn't about flooring, it was about distance. It was about credibility. It was about who was in and who wasn't.

At that moment, it clicked for me. *You're here, and this experience isn't going to come from the sidelines.*

As I paid more attention, I learned everyone in leadership was known as a carpet walker. That single nickname spoke volumes about how employees viewed management: well-intentioned, maybe, but disconnected. Observing rather than participating. Talking about the work instead of truly understanding it.

I couldn't ignore it.

I met with the leadership team one-by-one. I'd been working hard to earn their trust, and I knew this conversation would test it.

I started slowly, "Did you know the employees call us carpet walkers?"

A few laughed. Others shifted in their seats.

"If we want engagement to increase," I said, "we have to make a change in how we show up."

The nickname wasn't harmless, it was a signal. And if we ignored it, nothing would change. We needed less carpet, more concrete. Less distance. More presence.

From that point forward, I knew one thing for certain: if I was going to get this experience, I couldn't do it halfway. I had to immerse myself fully. Time wouldn't be the limiting factor; I was willing to live at the facility if that's what it took. This wasn't about punching a clock; it was about earning credibility.

I also knew how I felt about the company I worked for. I believed in it. I was proud to be there. And I wanted the employees in the facility to feel even a fraction of what I felt: to feel valued, respected, and part of something worth showing up for every day.

So instead of staying in my office, I hit the floor.

I came in at three in the morning to catch the night shift. I traded my heels for steel-toed boots. I shadowed employees, listened to what mattered to them, and learned how the work actually got done. I spent time with leaders too, not to point fingers or assign blame, but to understand the pressure they were under and to figure out how we could move forward together.

And slowly, things started to shift.

When the facility landed its first new business in decades, we celebrated. Who knew roll stock for a stick of butter could be so exciting? But it mattered. Sometimes it's the small wins that mean the most, especially for people who've shown up for decades without much to celebrate. For many of them, it had been a long time since anyone stopped to recognize progress. It just took an outside perspective to recognize this.

During all of this, I kept thinking about that tiny knob on Press 7. *How could something so small control something so critical?*

It became a powerful reminder: you can't support a business, or the people leading it, without understanding how the work actually happens.

Over the ten months I spent at that facility, something fundamental changed, not just in how others saw me, but in how I saw my role in HR.

Initially, I was unmistakably a carpet walker. But the more time I spent on the floor, the more the distance began to close. The nickname faded, not because anyone formally retired it, but because it stopped being true.

What I noticed first was trust. It didn't arrive all at once. It showed up in small ways, people explaining not just what they did, but why.

Leaders being more honest about what was and wasn't possible.

Employees invited me to lunch and to go ice fishing on the weekend, and asked questions they wouldn't have asked HR before.

Somewhere along the way, I stopped being "corporate HR" and became someone they believed was in it with them.

Personally, I felt different, too. It felt less like I was playing a role and more like I was doing meaningful work. I wasn't just there to roll out the latest performance management process or enforce policies; I was there to help solve real problems alongside real people.

By the time I left the facility, the impact was visible and measurable. Engagement scores increased by double digits. Leaders who struggled when I arrived found their footing, and many are still there today.

Those outcomes didn't come from a single initiative or tool; they came from showing up consistently, listening deeply, and earning credibility one conversation at a time.

On my last day, the team gave me a framed knob. It wasn't a thank-you for an HR initiative or a project milestone. It was recognition of a partnership, one built by meeting leaders where they were, standing next to them through uncertainty and some genuinely hard moments, and continuing to move the business forward together.

Before I left, they even let me start up Press 7, a long way from the early days of "Please don't touch anything."

When I look back on that experience, I realize it redefined how I think about my role in HR, and also helped me understand why our profession often gets a bad rap. I've heard it called the principal's office, the policy police, the fun committee, and let's not get started with Toby from *The Office*. We've been described as bureaucratic, administrative, and even overhead.

And if that's been your experience with HR, I believe you! But I'm also here to say: Something's not right.

What I learned is that these strained relationships usually aren't about bad intentions. Most business leaders don't set out to have an adversarial relationship with HR. Instead, both sides fall into a familiar and unproductive pattern. The disconnect usually sounds the same, just from different angles.

From the manager's perspective, HR can feel like a brick wall: the team that says no, asks for more documentation, or slows things down when pressure is already high.

From HR's perspective, managers often show up late in the process, already frustrated, and expect HR to "fix" a problem they're hearing about for the first time.

That disconnect creates finger-pointing instead of forward motion. And while it may be common, it doesn't serve the business.

The alternative is partnership.

In a true partnership, HR isn't a department you go to towards the end of a people problem. HR is someone you involve early, before decisions are locked in and options are limited. That shift requires effort on both sides.

Partnership starts with a mindset shift:

- View HR as your right hand, not a gatekeeper.
- Treat HR as an extension of your leadership team, not an external authority.

And since partnership goes both ways, HR must commit to understanding:

- How your business operates.
- What success looks like in each function.
- The talent, pressures, and constraints leaders are navigating every day.

When HR shows up as an employee first: curious, present, and invested, it earns the right to be a partner. When that relationship works, the question isn't whether HR adds value. It's how much more value becomes possible.

THE TOOL

After my experience at the manufacturing facility, I noticed the same dynamics repeatedly showed up in different organizations, industries, and leadership teams. The details changed, but the fundamentals didn't.

I wanted something I could return to in real time. Something simple enough to remember under pressure, but strong enough to change how leaders and HR work together. **M.E.E.T.** became the anchor. It's a way to meet people where they are, while still moving the business forward.

Each step has a purpose. When used together, they shift HR from a department leaders work around to a partner they rely on.

M-MAP BUSINESS REALITY

Before HR can be an effective partner, it has to understand the world leaders are operating in. This step establishes shared context and reduces the gap between strategy and execution.

Use this when HR seems disconnected from the business, when people solutions seem theoretical, or when decisions are being made without a clear understanding of operational pressure. If HR doesn't fully grasp how the business runs day to day, this is where to start.

Mapping the business reality means ensuring HR understands how the business operates, not just what's written in strategy decks or org charts. If your HR partner lacks business acumen, exclusion isn't the answer. Investment (on both sides) is.

This understanding is built through experience. As a leader, you play a critical role in closing this gap:

- Invite HR into operational conversations, not just people problems.
- Share financial realities, priorities, and trade-offs.
- Encourage HR to shadow key roles and learn workflows.
- Involve HR in projects, customer interactions, and strategic planning.
- Create space for questions and expect informed input.

HR Solutions fall apart when they are disconnected from business reality. When HR understands the pressure the business is under, their advice becomes practical instead of theoretical.

E-EARN TRUST THROUGH EARLY INVOLVEMENT

Nearly every business decision involves people, yet HR is at times brought in late, after decisions are made and options are limited.

Use this when decisions involve people, when leaders feel pressure to have everything "figured out" before asking for input, or when uncertainty exists, but urgency hasn't yet taken over.

Early involvement means bringing HR into conversations before decisions are finalized. Many leaders hesitate here, not because they don't value HR, but because they feel responsible for having answers. Under pressure, asking for input can feel like admitting uncertainty rather than practicing good leadership.

The problem is, waiting turns uncertainty into urgency, and urgency limits options. To earn trust through early involvement:

- Involve HR before decisions are locked in.
- Share context, not just conclusions.
- Use HR as a thinking partner, not an executor.
- Normalize asking for input as a part of strong leadership.

In its simplest form, the earlier HR is involved, the more options you have. Early involvement doesn't slow leadership. It gives leaders room to think, explore, and choose before the urgency removes that space.

E-EXPRESS THE PROBLEM IN BUSINESS TERMS

Progress slows when problems are softened, overcomplicated, or left unnamed. This step focuses on clarity, saying what's happening so the right solutions can follow.

Use this when something feels off but is hard to articulate, when leaders worry about saying the wrong thing, or when conversations feel overly complex or stuck.

Expressing the problem clearly doesn't require perfect language or HR jargon. It requires honesty. Leaders often over-filter their concerns, circling the issue instead of naming it, which slows progress and increases frustration on both sides.

Clarity, not polish, is what allows HR to help. When bringing an issue to HR:

- Speak plainly and honestly.
- Name what isn't working, even if it's uncomfortable.
- Think out loud without over-editing.
- Focus on clarity without losing respect.

When an issue is presented clearly, collaboration improves, emotions settle, and decisions are less likely to escalate prematurely.

T–TAILOR THE SOLUTION TOGETHER

Once the problem is clear, the real work begins. This step ensures solutions are shaped through partnership rather than handed off for execution.

Use this when a problem is clearly defined, and multiple paths forward exist, especially when leaders want outcomes, not just implementation.

Tailoring the solution together means the partnership doesn't stop at defining the problem. Leaders should come with a point of view, but not a one-time handoff. The best solutions are iterative, shaped through dialogue, testing assumptions, and shared accountability.

To design better solutions with HR:

- Share your perspective, then stay open.
- Expect HR to bring options, trade-offs, and alternatives.
- Revisit and refine solutions as conditions change.
- Treat implementation as a shared responsibility.

Nobody likes to scramble at the last minute to pull together a presentation or solution. This leaves room for error and little time for critical thinking or creativity. When leaders and HR design the solution together, there are limited last-minute scrambles and minimal second-guessing afterward.

MEETING IN THE MIDDLE

Each day when I sit at my desk, I see that framed knob. It doesn't remind me of a policy, a process, or a title. It reminds me of what happens when leaders and HR meet in the middle. When curiosity replaces assumptions, and partnership replaces finger-pointing.

When HR is used as a partner instead of a department, people's decisions stop feeling reactive. They become thoughtful, confident, and aligned with the business's direction.

So the next time something feels off, before frustration builds, before decisions solidify, pause and invite HR into the conversation.

M.E.E.T. them halfway. The business will move forward because of it.

Jaime Damkroger, MBA, PHR, is the founder of Talent Matters, where she partners with business owners and leaders to turn people challenges into business progress. Drawing on experience from large, complex organizations, Jaime specializes in translating proven people practices into practical, right-sized solutions that work for small and growing businesses.

With experience across manufacturing, financial services, and healthcare, Jaime is known for meeting leaders where they are and helping them use HR as a true business partner, not just a department. Throughout her career, she has worked alongside executives and leadership teams, navigating growth, engagement challenges, organizational change, and complex people decisions.

She brings a practical, human-centered lens to talent development, leadership effectiveness, and organizational design, helping businesses move forward without adding unnecessary complexity. Her work focuses on building trust between leaders and HR, creating clarity around people decisions, and designing solutions that fit the business, not the other way around.

Jaime was born and raised in Nebraska and holds an MBA from the University of Nebraska at Omaha. She is also a Professional in Human Resources (PHR). Outside of her work with leaders, Jaime spends her time shuttling her two kids to activities, exploring new vacation destinations with her family, walking her wheaten terrier Winnie, squeezing in a Pure Barre class, and enjoying a good book.

Connect with Jaime:

If you're unsure whether your HR function is truly operating as a business partner, or simply a supporting activity, you can assess it directly. Take the **HR Business Impact Assessment** at the link below to identify where HR is driving value in your organization, and where it may be falling short.

Website: https://alltalentmatters.com/meet

LinkedIn: https://www.linkedin.com/in/jaimedamkroger/

CHAPTER 11

ZERO TO SIX FIGURES

CLARITY CREATES DIRECTION.
RELATIONSHIPS OPEN DOORS.

Brooke Toomey

MY STORY

I didn't know my marriage was ending that night, but my body did.

I lay awake night after night and stared at the ceiling. My mind raced with one terrifying question: *How am I going to make ends meet?* I wasn't leaving a marriage alone. I had two daughters in elementary school who depended on me, and I had no work history after more than ten years as a stay-at-home mom.

My bachelor's degree offered little help in supporting a family. I had dreams I wasn't willing to abandon—dreams that required more than survival wages. The most important of those dreams had been missing from my life for a very long time, and that was travel.

Twenty-three years earlier, while living alone in Spain, I learned that travel made my heart sing. It expanded my worldview. It softened my judgments. It made me a more grounded, compassionate human. It became part of who I was at my core—and it was a gift I longed to give my children. I wanted them to grow up with open minds and open hearts toward people who were different from them.

Before I ever said, "I do," I explained how essential travel was to my happiness.

"I want to make sure you know that travel is essential to my happiness. It's something I need for us to do together." I said.

"Are you kidding?! When I lived in Germany, I traveled throughout Europe almost every weekend. I love that you want to travel! We can make this happen."

After the vows were spoken and the ring was on my finger, I learned his words were empty.

"Please," I said year after year. "This matters to me. I'm home with our kids every day. I need something that makes me feel like myself. I can't live like this."

"There isn't enough money," he responded.

"But we give ten percent of your pre-tax income away. Could we lower that so I can do what makes me want to get out of bed in the morning?"

"Do you really think that's what we should be spending money on?" he asked. "Vacations instead of supporting what matters most?"

That conversation repeated itself for years.

The message was always the same—what mattered to him would always come first.

Money was always available for what mattered to him, but there was never enough for me. My needs went unheard. My voice felt invisible in my own life. As the days turned into years, I became deeply depressed—and slowly, quietly, I fell out of love.

One night in 2014, lying beside him in bed after the same argument yet again, something shifted.

When he said, "There just isn't enough money," the fight drained out of me. He wasn't trying to hurt me. But I saw then that my needs would never matter in the way they needed to.

I realized: *I can't keep disappearing inside this life.*

That was the first time divorce entered my mind.

The next day, I scheduled an emergency appointment with my therapist.

"I'm thinking about divorce for the first time," I told her through tears. "I don't want to feel this way. I don't know what to do. I feel overwhelmed, angry, and completely hopeless."

She paused, then said, "Let's start helping you build a life where you can support yourself—whether you stay or leave."

The first step was clarity.

I had no idea what I wanted to do, only that I needed a path forward. Through a series of career-discovery exercises, I identified what might support the life I wanted to build. That's when human resources emerged as a possible field that aligned with my strengths and could provide both stability and growth.

One exercise she assigned me was something I'd never heard of before: an informational interview.

I searched LinkedIn for an HR director in my area and found a woman named Lauren. I cold messaged her: "Would you be willing to talk with me about your career?" She said yes!

During that conversation, I asked questions. I listened. I learned. And for the first time, I pictured myself in a future role. The work sounded meaningful. The path felt real. I left that conversation knowing I was headed in the right direction.

Soon after, I secured a part-time recruiting job I could do from home—work that didn't disrupt my responsibilities with the kids. I wasn't earning much, but something important happened. My travel fund began to grow slowly. More importantly, so did my résumé.

One night, scrolling Facebook, I saw Southwest Airlines advertising $39 flights to the Bahamas. With airfare that cheap, I could afford a modest hotel. My husband had to work, so I took the kids alone.

Just my girls and me.

Those five days were the happiest I experienced in over a decade. I felt alive again. And somewhere between ocean swims and shared laughter, I realized something quiet but unmistakably true: I'd be happier—and better able to provide for my children—on my own.

On Valentine's Day in 2016, my husband chose to attend an optional overnight work event after I asked him to stay home. In that moment, I knew. My needs would never be his priority—but I had to start making them mine.

With a part-time job, the clothes on our backs, and my two daughters beside me, I left without a plan—only the certainty that staying would cost me everything.

I built a résumé from scratch and applied for jobs.

I came across a position that felt like a dream step toward my goals—a role that allowed me to gain experience in every area of human resources. I wanted it badly. But even as I prepared for the interview, I knew I wasn't yet the candidate they were looking for. The interview itself went well, but my lack of experience ultimately stood in the way. The hiring manager, Dan, was kind and honest when he told me, "You're not quite ready."

Before leaving, I asked, "Can I keep in touch?"

Every few months, I sent a short LinkedIn message—never asking for anything, simply checking in and sharing what I was working on professionally.

Meanwhile, I took whatever work I could find.

At that stage of my life, my career looked anything but stable. I moved between part-time, temporary, and entry-level roles. Paychecks fluctuated. Titles came and went. There were moments I questioned: *Am I moving forward at all?!*

But underneath the volatility of my work, one thing remained steady: I stayed connected.

While catering an event one evening, I ran into a woman who had worked in my high school office decades earlier. She worked in HR at the Board of Education. "I'm pursuing an HR career," I told her. "Send your résumé!" she said.

A minimum-wage temp role opened at the front desk that summer. I accepted without hesitation.

At thirty-eight, I shared front-desk duties with a twenty-year-old college student—and I didn't care. I wasn't chasing titles or ego. I was building credibility.

When that role ended, the organization continued placing me in temporary positions because of my work ethic. Eventually, I realized I had drifted away from my long-term goal of becoming an HR leader.

So, I refocused.

The hotel job I once interviewed for reopened. I reached out to Dan. He remembered me. "I'd be happy to interview you," he said. This time, I had experience—and the relationship mattered.

I got the job.

That role changed everything. As an HR department of one, I learned every aspect of the field. Under Dan's mentorship as a regional HR director, my career accelerated.

Two years later, ready for my next challenge, I noticed an opening at Lauren's company—the same woman who once provided an informational interview with me years earlier. I reached out. Two weeks later, I received an offer.

Lauren didn't just open one door for me. Over time, she offered me three separate opportunities, all because I stayed in touch. All because I kept checking in without asking for anything in return.

Then came the moment that changed my financial life forever.

I reached out to an old high school acquaintance—someone I'd stayed loosely connected to over the years. He introduced me to someone who interviewed me. Three hours later, I had a six-figure job offer.

It felt sudden, but actually, it was an opportunity years in the making.

Looking back, every pivotal career moment came from a relationship I nurtured quietly and consistently. I didn't network loudly. I didn't make transactional asks. I followed up. I remembered people. I let trust compound while I did the work in front of me.

Five years after starting from zero, I became the head of an HR department, earning six figures.

In 2021, standing in the humid rainforest of Costa Rica, tears streaming down my face as spider monkeys swung overhead, I realized something profound.

I'm here because I built this life myself.

My jobs were temporary. My relationships were not.

I got clear

I stayed focused.

And I maintained the connections that opened every door along the way.

When people rise, it's rarely because of a single bold leap or a perfect opportunity. More often, it happens through small, intentional choices repeated over time.

Looking back, my career didn't change because I worked harder or found a hidden shortcut. It changed because I learned how to combine clarity with connection. The most pivotal moments in my story didn't come from applications or timing—they came from conversations.

Conversations that helped me understand my direction.

Conversations that built trust.

Conversations that opened doors long before I ever needed them.

Those conversations began with one simple tool: the informational interview.

THE TOOL

THE INFORMATIONAL INTERVIEW

When people hear *From Zero to Six Figures*, they often assume there's a secret résumé format, a perfect certification, or a magical job board that makes it happen.

There isn't.

What actually creates career momentum—especially during a pivot—is clarity paired with connection. It's knowing what direction you want to move in and building relationships with people already walking that path. That's where informational interviews come in.

As an HR leader for over a decade, I can say this with complete honesty: most jobs are filled long before they're ever posted. Many of the people hired were not the most impressive on paper; they were the most trusted. Informational interviews are often where that trust begins.

An informational interview is a short, low-pressure conversation with someone who works in a role, company, or industry you're curious about. It's not a job interview. You're not asking for a position. You're asking for insight.

Think of it as career research—but human. Instead of guessing what a role is really like from job descriptions, you learn directly from someone doing the work every day.

For people starting over, the greatest obstacle is rarely skill. It's uncertainty. You may find yourself thinking, *I don't know what I want to do anymore,* or *I can't afford another wrong move.* Every job posting begins to sound the same, and decision fatigue sets in.

Informational interviews cut through that fog.

They help you understand what the work actually looks like, which skills matter most, how people truly entered the field, and which paths you didn't even know existed. Just as importantly, they allow others to remember you—not as an applicant, but as a person.

Careers don't pivot on applications; they pivot on relationships.

Clarity alone doesn't create income, and connection without clarity doesn't either. But when the two come together, momentum builds. One conversation leads to another. That conversation leads to insight, a referral, a recommendation, a contract role, or a job that never appears online. Informational interviews rarely feel powerful in the moment, but they compound quietly over time.

To begin, look for people in roles you're curious about, companies you admire, or positions one or two steps ahead of where you want to be. These conversations don't require a warm connection. LinkedIn, alumni networks, former coworkers, and mutual contacts are more than enough.

When reaching out, keep your message simple and human. Share that you're exploring a career direction and would value twenty minutes of insight. Including language like *"no job ask—just hoping to learn"* removes pressure and dramatically increases your chances of hearing "Yes."

Prepare a few thoughtful questions in advance. Ask what a typical day looks like, what surprised them most about the role, which skills truly matter, and what they would do differently if starting again. Early conversations should focus on understanding the work, not salary or titles.

During the conversation, listen more than you speak. You're not there to impress. You're there to learn.

Before ending, ask one powerful question:
Is there anyone else you'd recommend I speak with?

That single question often opens the next door.

Always send a thank-you note within twenty-four hours. Reference something specific you learned and express appreciation for their time. This simple step is where many relationships either fade or deepen.

If you're rebuilding after divorce, burnout, layoffs, or years away from the workforce, informational interviews offer something invaluable: confidence rooted in knowledge.

You stop guessing.

You stop chasing random job postings.

You stop feeling behind.

Instead, you begin making intentional decisions based on clarity rather than fear. That's how direction forms. And direction, supported by relationships, opens doors that résumés alone never will.

Because no one goes from zero to six figures alone.

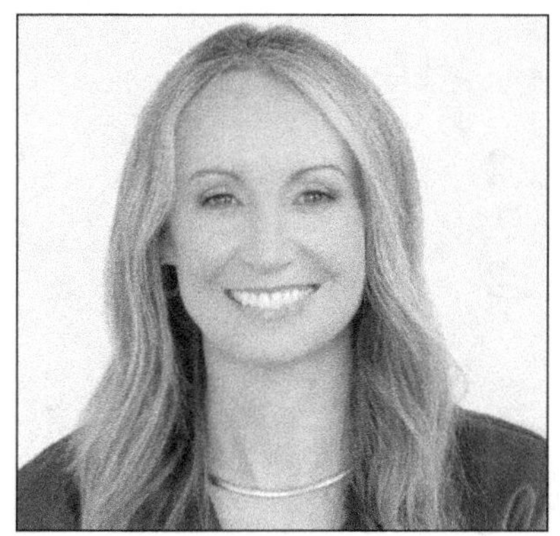

Brooke Toomey is a career coach, former HR executive, and the founder of **Her Perfect Career**, a coaching practice focused on helping women build meaningful, financially stable careers that align with the lives they want—not just the résumés they have.

With more than a decade of experience in human resources leadership across multiple industries, Brooke brings a behind-the-scenes understanding of how hiring decisions are truly made.

Today, she supports women navigating workforce reentry, career pivots, burnout recovery, and rebuilding after divorce. Her work centers on clarity, confidence, and sustainable growth—helping clients design careers that support both income goals and life priorities.

After building a six-figure HR career within five years of reentering the workforce, Brooke founded Her Perfect Career to make practical, human-centered career guidance accessible to women ready for more.

Brooke lives in Annapolis, Maryland, with her two daughters and her six-pound Shih Tzu–Pomeranian mix. Outside of work, she is passionate about travel, nature, wildlife, and experiencing new cultures—especially through food from around the world. From time to time, you'll find her out-of-office reply turned on while she's living her long-held dream of travel and time outdoors.

Connect with Brooke:

Website: http://www.herperfectcareer.com/

Connect: http://www.herperfectcareer.com/contact

Email: brooke@herperfectcareer.com

CHAPTER 12

THE SOLO SEAT AT THE TABLE

USING CONVERSATION TO DRIVE REAL HR CHANGE

Ben Madden

MY STORY

I kept telling myself the same thing: *Don't let them see you sweat.*

I was twenty-three when I walked into my first HR lead role—as a consultant. Young, ambitious, and full of theory, I sat at the table with senior leaders twice my age, tasked with "fixing HR." I had a client list, a project scope, and the quiet panic that comes with being the one expected to have all the answers.

What I didn't have: peers, a blueprint, or even someone to bounce ideas off. I was, in every sense, an HR Department of one.

My early days were a blur of policy rewrites, filing (always filing!), and carefully navigating HR tasks I had never encountered before. I learned on the fly. My HR "education" was one class in college and an internship. Every decision felt like it had stakes. One slip, and I imagined the whole house of cards would fall. *One slip and this entire company could fall apart. I can't take it.*

But I learned fast. I had to. When things didn't go well, I assumed it was 100% my fault and felt the weight of it. I even handed in my resignation at one point over something that, looking back, I'd consider a minor issue that was easily fixable.

FROM START-UP BURNOUT TO BURN-IN

After years of consulting, I moved in-house at a high-growth startup. We scaled fast and burned people out even quicker. Layoffs were made at the end of every quarter. It was an *always-on* culture. People my age ran the company and had no idea how to manage.

It was the most challenging role of my career. Not because of the volume—but because I watched people break. And no one thought to ask HR if *I* was okay. All the video games, ping-pong, and other "entrepreneurial" perks didn't change the fact that the developers were struggling to keep up with the owners' demands. Nothing was ever going fast enough in any department. I even tried instituting half-day Fridays to help with burnout, but eventually, no one took the time off because they were too swamped with work.

Eventually, I burned out too. Bringing myself to work was tough; I felt hopeless. There were days when I could barely get anything done, and dragging myself to work was a chore unto itself, as I knew that the next problem was right around the corner or the next layoff was imminent. And when I left, they scrapped nearly everything I built within days (and then fired the consultant they brought in to replace me). I knew that the two years of work I felt enthusiastic about were gone in an instant.

But here's the thing: that start-up taught me how *not* to build. And sometimes, knowing what doesn't work is the most powerful lesson of all. These lessons continue to this day: hiring your friends and family can be difficult when tough conversations are needed, micromanagement isn't an effective leadership tool, hiring people who are willing to challenge you is key, and, frankly, the list goes on and on.

REBUILDING—WITH PURPOSE

Next came an internal role where I was trusted to lead a team of two. I had a seat, a voice, and the space to think long-term. But the industry hit a downturn, and one by one, the team disappeared. Eventually, it was just me again—scrappy, solo, and building the HR function from the ground up. We had times when the team would grow, and then, sure enough, the next bump in the road: "Ben, we need to cut HR staff."

This time, though, I was ready. I focused on impact. I tied HR work to meet business outcomes. I trained leaders, improved compliance, and maintained a relentless focus on employee experience.

I became indispensable. And that mattered. We won Best Places to Work through hard work and my desire to make a profound impact.

FINDING MY PEOPLE

Over the years, I've built HR infrastructure for companies ranging from 5 to 250 employees across government contracting, nonprofits, and startups. I guided orgs through their first hires, helped them leave expensive Professional Employer Organizations, and transitioned them into full-time HR leadership.

But somewhere in those years, I realized what I was missing: connection. As HR pros, we carry so much on our own. So, I leaned into community—first with the Northern Virginia Society of Human Resource Management chapter, even becoming President twice, then by helping relaunch DisruptHR DC (a biannual HR speaker series with an international brand).

I found the spaces I wish I had when I started and made a difference. We cannot be Superman and do it all, all the time.

And now? I love **coaching new HR leaders so they don't have to go it alone.**

WHAT I BELIEVE NOW

The best organizations I've worked with all share a few things:

- They *actually* value their people. Not just in branding—but in budget, behavior, and accountability.
- They see HR as a strategic lever, not a necessary evil.
- They trust their people leaders and invest in making them better.
- They operate with radical transparency and mutual accountability.

And the best HR leaders? They know the job isn't to have all the answers—it's to ask the right questions.

That's why I created the tool below: a simple conversation framework that helps leaders connect people strategy to business strategy.

THE TOOL

THE STRATEGIC CONVERSATION FRAMEWORK: REFRAMING HR DIALOGUE

Over the years, I've found that many HR leaders (including me) struggle not because we lack expertise, but because we're stuck in the wrong kind of conversations. We're fighting for budgets, compliance alignment, or policy changes in rooms where we're seen as back-office support rather than strategic partners.

So, I built a simple framework to help shift those conversations.

This tool isn't fancy. It's just a set of questions. But used consistently, it helps HR leaders shift from being seen as "the people person" to becoming indispensable partners in solving business problems.

STEP 1: WHAT'S THE BUSINESS OBJECTIVE?

"Before we even talk about headcount or benefits, what's the bigger business goal we're trying to accomplish?"

Every strategic HR conversation starts here. If you're not clear on the company's goals—growth targets, contract wins, new market expansion, operational efficiencies—then you're building in a vacuum.

Example: A CEO says they need to "hire faster." But when I ask this question, I learn they're trying to win a re-compete with a tighter labor margin. Suddenly, it's not just about recruiting—it's about redesigning roles, comp strategy, and subcontractor mix to preserve margin.

STEP 2: WHAT HAS TO HAPPEN WITH PEOPLE TO MAKE THAT POSSIBLE?

"To hit that goal, what would people need to do differently?"

This is where HR becomes a multiplier. Once the business goal is clear, translate it into people's actions. Are we scaling? Then, onboarding and org design are the keys. Are we reducing risk? Then it's policy clarity and manager training.

Example: A government contractor I supported was expanding into a new contract vehicle. The business need was speed. But without straightforward onboarding and manager alignment, new hires were churning in three months. We rebuilt the onboarding with role-specific checklists, clearer task ownership, and manager accountability. Retention doubled in six months.

STEP 3: WHAT SYSTEMS OR STRUCTURES ARE HELPING OR HURTING?

"Do our current systems (policies, tech, workflows) support this goal, or block it?"

This is where the hard truth comes in. Sometimes we're protecting outdated systems because "that's how we've always done it." This question permits you to name what's broken, or at least misaligned.

Example: When I was internal, we had great talent, but performance reviews were annual, vague, and delayed. The CEO didn't trust the ratings, and promotions felt random. We moved to a quarterly feedback loop tied to project metrics and gave managers a simple 1-pager for quarterly career conversations. Engagement and trust jumped within one cycle.

STEP 4: WHAT WILL SUCCESS LOOK LIKE, AND HOW WILL WE MEASURE IT?

"What numbers, stories, or signals will tell us we're on the right track?"

You don't need to be a data scientist. But you do need clarity. Are we reducing time-to-fill? Increasing first-year retention? Seeing fewer compliance misses? Define success early, and revisit it often.

Example: At a fast-scaling startup, the founder asked me to "fix HR." That's not a metric. Instead, we defined success as: reducing regrettable turnover, improving Glassdoor reviews, and building manager confidence in handling performance issues. Six months in, those metrics told the story far better than any HR dashboard ever could.

HOW TO USE THE FRAMEWORK IN PRACTICE

Here's what I've learned: the magic isn't in the framework itself. It's in **using it consistently.** Not in every meeting. But in the moments where stakes are high— budget reviews, strategy off-sites, or anytime a leader says, "HR needs to fix this."

TACTICAL WAYS TO EMBED IT:

- Prep for exec 1:1s by walking yourself through the questions
- Use the four questions to structure HR project proposals
- Train HR business partners to use the framework with department heads
- Introduce it in People Strategy off-sites as a way to align HR initiatives with business OKRs (Objectives and Key Results—a way to measure organizational success)

And when in doubt? Bring the questions into the room.

"Before we dive in, can we zoom out for a second? What's the bigger objective here, and how do we think people need to show up differently to get there?"

That one sentence can change how people see HR, not as the function that slows things down, but as the one that gets the business unstuck.

Ben Madden is the founder of HR Action, where he serves as a fractional Chief People Officer to leadership teams navigating growth, complexity, and increased scrutiny. His work focuses on helping organizations identify people, compliance, and leadership risks before they surface during scale, audits, or transitions.

Over the past 20 years, Ben has led HR for organizations ranging from early-stage startups to $50M+ enterprises—often as an HR department of one operating at the executive level. That experience shaped his philosophy: HR is not administrative support, but business infrastructure. When people's decisions aren't intentionally designed as companies grow, risk compounds quietly and becomes expensive later.

Ben partners closely with founders, CEOs, and operators to design people strategy, decision frameworks, and systems that actually hold up under growth. His work spans regulated and high-scrutiny environments as well as fast-moving, founder-led organizations. He has guided companies through PEO exits, reduced insurance and benefits costs by double digits, and built a scalable people infrastructure that supports growth from five employees to 200+, with a people strategy directly tied to business outcomes.

In addition to his advisory work, Ben is a frequent speaker and facilitator, including appearances at DisruptHR, NEXCO, and other events.

Ben lives and works in Arlington, VA, and is passionate about helping organizations scale without losing clarity, accountability, or trust.

Connect with Ben:

Website: http://www.hractionllc.com/

LinkedIn: https://www.linkedin.com/in/benmadden/

WHAT ACTUALLY WORKS

SYSTEMS THAT SUPPORT GROWTH AND SUCCESS

CHAPTER 13

CONNECTION FUELS GROWTH

HOW PEOPLE POWER YOUR BRAND'S SUCCESS

Stacey Piper, Fractional Chief Marketing Officer

MY STORY

I gave sixteen years of my life to that company. Sixteen years!

I walked out of his office reeling. My hands were clammy, slick with sweat, and my heart pounded so loudly I was sure someone in the hallway could hear it. *Did that actually just happen?* I replayed the conversation on a loop as I rode the empty elevator down to the floor where my office had been for three years, since my promotion to Vice President of Marketing.

"I'm certain you'll be working half as much and making twice as much next time I talk to you," he said casually—almost breezily—as he turned his chair back toward his desk and returned to his work.

I was stunned—rendered speechless. This was my career, my life's work!

How could he be so dismissive, and simultaneously so positive and confident that I'd land on my feet?

I carried a cardboard box of belongings to my car, his words echoing in my mind. With a mix of grief and quiet anger, I realized my farewell to the CEO I worked for all those years ended not with reassurance, not with gratitude, not with explanation or comfort—but with what felt like him easing his own conscience about my departure.

The days that followed blurred together. Then weeks. Then months. I watched my life from outside my body. I moved like a robot—waking up, showering, putting on makeup, seeing my family off to work and school. Once the house fell silent, I sat alone in the dark, heavy with pain, asking myself the same questions over and over.

What did I do to deserve this? How could a company that I gave so much to not recognize my value?

I searched for jobs mechanically. I reconnected with people in my network—not because I had a clear plan, but because connection was the only thing that still felt real. I applied for position after position. Occasionally, I forced myself out of the house—walking the dogs, running errands, meeting someone for coffee or lunch—smiling politely while feeling hollow inside.

At four o'clock every afternoon, I put my brave face back on. School pickup. Playtime. Dinner. Cleanup. Bedtime routines. Then, long after the house was quiet, I lay awake staring at the ceiling, trapped in relentless questions about my own self-worth.

Around the three-month mark, the calls started coming—interviews— good ones. The roles were interesting enough, and the titles impressive enough, that I imagined my bruised ego healing once my LinkedIn profile reflected my worth again.

But no offers came.

The roles weren't going to someone else. The companies—large, bureaucratic organizations—were simply slow. Slow to decide. Slow to commit. Slow to move.

One day, while venting to a headhunter friend, she determinedly emphasized, "You were in sales. You know how to close the deal. Just ask the hiring manager, 'What's it going to take to get this job?'"

And in that moment, a quiet truth surfaced.

I don't want the job.

I paused, confused.

Had I just been doing what I thought was expected of me? Was I simply trying for the big job title to validate my existence?

Back to square one. *What do I want?*

I realized I was happiest working for a small, fast-growth firm—like the one I had just spent sixteen years at, nurturing it into the global brand. One without silos or red tape—a place where relationships mattered more than org charts. Where people talked to each other, helped each other, and stepped in (even stepped up) where help was needed. Where anyone brave enough to raise their hand, solve a problem, and fill a gap was rewarded with ownership.

I wanted to create a role like the one my boss had when I joined that now billion-dollar brand sixteen years earlier.

With renewed purpose—and a flicker of fire in my belly—I returned to my network. This time, not just asking for jobs, but for conversations. For introductions. For perspective. I met with several small-government-contractor CEOs. With some, I truly clicked. We whiteboarded roles, mapped responsibilities, and talked openly about what their businesses needed and where they were headed.

But it was a transition year for the administration, and government funding was uncertain. None of them were willing—or able—to invest in a strategic leader they hadn't planned for.

Then one of them said something that stopped me cold.

"When you start consulting," she said lightheartedly, "let us know."

It wasn't a job offer. It was a connection. An open door. And a spark!

I reflected. *It's not the first time someone has made this suggestion. In fact, didn't my former CEO say the very same thing just four months earlier?*

I never seriously considered a consulting career. I was always comfortable working within structure, building value for someone else. Still, that comment stayed with me, echoing in my head.

That weekend, my husband and I went out to dinner. He works in finance and has always been my clearest, calmest sounding board. Tentatively, I asked, "If I were to consult, what income would I need to bring home so we don't have to change our spending or saving habits?"

Ever the accountant, he asked, "Give me a few days to run the numbers."

When we revisited the topic a few days later, he gave me a five-digit figure. It was reasonable—shockingly so. "Yes! I know I can do this!"

Then I asked the harder question. "How long do I have?"

"Six months," he said.

With that, I had a target. And I had hope.

I went back to my network again—this time with an entirely different ask: *What do I need to do to build something of my own?* My connections came through in spades—openly sharing their knowledge and experience. I registered an LLC, opened a bank account, secured insurance, bought a URL, built a website, updated my LinkedIn profile, and let people know I had officially hung my own shingle.

But more importantly, I started reactivating my network, reconnecting with intention. Not pitching. Not selling. Just talking—connecting with intention. I let people know what I was trying to create and how I might help.

It was a long slog.

For six months, I wrote blogs, published newsletters, ran email campaigns, and stayed visible. I networked with purpose—both digitally and in-person. Not transactionally, but relationally. Checking in, following up, and offering value where I could. I tapped into my natural curiosity, asking questions, intently listening, and engaging. I did pro bono work for nonprofits to stay sharp, to stay useful, and to remind myself that contribution still mattered.

Then, in December, I heard back from a prospective client I had been introduced to months earlier. I hadn't chased him. I nurtured the new relationship by sharing valuable content and demonstrating genuine interest—simply staying in connection. When he responded to my latest outreach to tell me he was finally ready to start, it felt like validation—not just of my skills, but of my authenticity.

I had no idea what to charge. His business was shrinking. He had just laid off thirty people, one-third of his team.

I sold my first consulting contract as a twelve-month retainer. The total came to exactly the number my husband had calculated.

I took a deep breath and held it.

I paused in near disbelief. *I did it. I really did it.*

I hit the target—and it was within the six months. And so, a new chapter began.

That first engagement ran beautifully. The client was generous, engaged, and collaborative. I attended on-site meetings, joined team events, and was even invited to attend holiday parties and participate in service projects. They didn't treat me like a vendor; they treated me like a trusted partner.

Then something unexpected happened.

A former coworker reached out—someone who knew how I worked, how I led, and how I showed up for people. "The company I'm consulting for needs your help." She introduced me to the CEO. That introduction turned into meetings, then trust, then another client.

Now I had two clients. The second needed more work, faster, but it required specialized expertise I didn't have. So I did what got me here in the first place.

I leaned into connection.

I called former colleagues—people I trusted, people whose work I respected, people who were also impacted by job eliminations. The band was back together, not because of titles or contracts, but because of shared history and mutual trust.

That project was a success. And something bigger happened alongside it.

I wasn't just building a client base. I was rebuilding a community.

Momentum followed—clients in Virginia and Maryland, subcontractors who became collaborators, clients who became subcontractors, vendors who became partners, relationships that deepened with every shared win. I didn't hit the numbers my former CEO predicted, but I exceeded every goal my husband and I set for my business.

Toward the end of my first full year in business, another former colleague called. He had landed in a growth role and needed help. "The company I work for just got a new website, but something's not right. I'm the Chief Growth Officer, and I don't want to fail. I know you can help us." I listened closely, asked questions, and created a new service offering based entirely on what his company needed—even though I didn't yet know how to deliver it. I knew someone who did. We met at an industry conference five years earlier. So I made the call.

That friend said yes. He still works with me today.

My former colleague left that company, but the company remains my client eight years later.

My pulse quickened. *That was the moment it all crystallized.*

My consultancy didn't succeed through winning bids and responding to job postings. It grew through connection.

A sense of quiet calm came over me. Some glorious truths manifested.

Clients came from relationships.

Subcontractors came from trust.

Opportunities came from staying visible, helpful, and human.

And that was when I finally grasped it. My former CEO was right.

I will work half as much. I will make twice as much.

But more importantly, I will never work alone again.

And it would be *oh, so* rewarding.

EIGHT YEARS LATER

Today, I run a vibrant, successful communications and marketing consultancy. And what I learned then still holds true now: growth happens through connection—real human connection—between people.

Despite how dramatically my corporate career life ended, I built a strong, trusted relationship with the CEO I worked for during those sixteen years. In fact, he remains a strong advocate and reference. And I spent nearly two decades alongside talented colleagues, leaders, and partners, and together we became a respected, recognizable brand. Those relationships—and the credibility that came from being a dependable part of that ecosystem—became some of my most productive and valuable assets.

The connections I formed there didn't disappear when I walked out the door. They evolved. Former colleagues became future clients. Trusted peers became collaborators and subcontractors. Deep relationships built over years of shared work, pressure, and success turned into opportunities I could've never planned for—but was ready to step into.

That belief shapes how I build teams, serve clients, partner with subcontractors, and attract talent, for my own firm and for my clients' firms.

People don't connect with offerings. They connect with people.

And when you design your business—your marketing, brand, and culture—around that core principle, everything changes.

WHAT I LEARNED

Over the course of my career—and especially after starting my own firm—I began to notice a pattern.

The opportunities that changed everything didn't come from formal job postings, brilliant RFP (requests for proposals) responses, polished pitches, or perfectly worded capability statements. They came from people—former colleagues, trusted peers, leaders who remembered how it felt to work together. People who knew how I showed up, not just what I could do.

Connection was doing the real work.

At first, I didn't have language for it. I just knew that every meaningful inflection point in my career was tied to a relationship: someone willing to make an introduction, take a chance, collaborate, or say, "Let's build this together."

Over time, I realized this wasn't accidental. It was a deliberate construct, one that most companies fail to implement.

Many organizations believe growth is driven by offerings, systems, and scale. And while those things matter, they're not what people remember. People remember how you made them feel, whether you showed up. Whether you listened. Whether you saw them as more than a transaction.

THE TOOL

That realization led me to develop what I now call the **B.R.I.D.G. Framework™**.

At its core, the philosophy reflects two truths.

1. Growth depends on building connections—both inside and outside the organization.

2. Connection has depth. Some interactions are purely functional. Others are deeply relational. The strongest brands intentionally invest in both.

Growth happens when your internal and external systems are symbiotic. When culture, credibility, authority, and impact fire in sync—it is the impetus for driving connected, sustainable growth. When you map these dimensions together, four distinct zones emerge.

One reflects what it feels like to work within your organization—**belonging**. Another reflects how the market experiences your humanity and point of view—**reputation**. A third shows how work actually gets done—**integrity** of operations. And the fourth reveals how your people create impact for clients, partners, and communities—**delivery**.

Organizations fail when there's a disconnect between internal culture and external impact. Most companies operate in only one or two of these zones. They may be operationally strong but culturally disconnected. Or visible in the market but hollow internally.

The result? Friction. Burnout. Churn. Stalled growth.

Growth follows when signals move cleanly across all four. Companies can expect that if they nourish these elements in tandem—intentionally and consistently—a powerful inflection happens.

Former colleagues become future collaborators.

Employees become advocates.

Clients become partners.

And growth stops feeling forced and high-pressure, starts feeling earned and organic.

Add to that, marketing as a force multiplier. Demonstrate externally that building bridges and forging connections matter to your organization to realize true acceleration.

To illustrate how it feels to work for a compelling brand, present your people, values, and culture on social media and recruitment websites. A sense of **belonging** can be portrayed by highlighting relationships and connections. **People stay where they feel valued.**

To showcase **reputation** and demonstrate human brand authority, publish thought-leadership content featuring subject matter experts sharing their insights. **Real people sharing real insights builds credibility.**

To demonstrate the **integrity** of operations, highlight the investments your firm makes in tools and training for your people. Show how you do this by rewarding staff publicly for earning certifications and awards. **Strong systems empower strong people.**

To drive home market impact present examples of exemplary **delivery**, release images and stories about your alliances with partners and support of community organizations on your website and social media. **What you deliver matters—and how—matters even more. Impact is where trust becomes tangible.**

This methodology isn't a human resources or marketing communications framework. It's a leadership one.

It's a way to see your brand not as a logo or a message, but as a living network of people. People connected by trust, shared experience, and purpose.

And when you put people at the center, growth follows.

B.R.I.D.G. FRAMEWORK DIAGNOSTIC CHECKLIST

Ask yourself: *Which Quadrants Are You Under-Investing In?*

INSTRUCTIONS:

SCORE EACH STATEMENT FROM 1 (NOT TRUE AT ALL) TO 5 (CONSISTENTLY TRUE).

TALLY SCORES BY QUADRANT.

Quadrant 1: Belonging *(Internal + Relational)*

- Employees feel recognized and valued beyond their job titles.
- Leadership communicates openly and consistently.
- We honor and highlight our people internally and externally.
- Former employees remain connected to our brand.
- Employees refer candidates because they're proud of where they work.

Score Range: 5–25

Quadrant 2: Reputation *(External + Relational)*

- Our thought leadership is led by real people, not just the brand logo.
- Subject matter experts are visible and supported—not muted or hidden.
- Our content reflects experience and perspective, not just capabilities and solutions.
- Prospects engage with us before a sales conversation ever begins.
- People reference our point of view when they talk about us.

Score Range: 5–25

Quadrant 3: Integrity of Operations *(Internal + Functional)*

- Our processes are clear, repeatable, and people enabled.
- Teams understand how their work connects to outcomes.
- We invest in onboarding, mentoring, and enablement.
- Case studies reflect team contributions, not just results.
- We scale without burning people out.

Score Range: 5–25

Quadrant 4: Delivery *(External + Functional)*

- Clients understand how we work—not just what we deliver.
- We recognize partners and subcontractors externally.
- Our community involvement reflects our values and ties to our mission.
- We co-create success stories with clients.
- Partners prioritize us because they trust our people.

Score Range: 5–25

INTERPRETING RESULTS BY QUADRANT

20-25: STRENGTH—KEEP INVESTING

14-19: INCONSISTENT—OPPORTUNITY FOR FOCUSED INVESTMENT

BELOW 14: GROWTH RISK—UNDER-INVESTED QUADRANT

Quotient measures the magnitude of something. The higher the quotient, the better. With this diagnostic checklist, the higher your score, the higher your connection quotient. The higher your CQ, the more likely your company can achieve sustainable **growth**.

For the B.R.I.D.G. Framework to fuel growth, you must have these four zones of connection:

- **What:** A connected point of view, one with market authority based on collective thought leadership and experience
- **Why:** A connected mindset, all driving toward clients' desired outcomes
- **How:** A connected process, one that is reliable for delivery and achieving outcomes
- **Who:** A connected culture where ideas are shared in an open, trusting environment

This is how companies build bridges to grow a brand that triumphs. Growth isn't an output; it's an energy you cultivate and synchronize across these four zones.

If this resonates with you, and you want to know more about your company's connection quotient and how to raise it, **let's connect!**

Stacey Piper is a seasoned marketing communications leader with more than 30 years of experience helping firms elevate their brand and accelerate growth. She is known for transforming marketing into a force multiplier—aligning strategy, storytelling, and execution to connect purpose to performance.

Stacey modernizes communications departments and optimizes marketing operations to deliver bold, human-centered strategies that resonate. She provides fractional CMO and integrated outsourced marketing services, working hands-on as a trusted advisor and mentor while building scalable solutions and in-house capacity for firms. She helps firms navigate inflection points in growth and identity by shifting messaging, organizational and talent models, and the systems and processes required for long-term success.

Stacey has built and led high-impact marketing programs that educate, increase awareness, and enhance brand familiarity across competitive markets. Her expertise spans brand strategy, digital marketing, thought leadership, and demand generation to strengthen human interaction, trust, and long-term client relationships.

In her time leading MarCom organizations, she partnered closely with HR leaders and executive leadership to drive effective M&A communications as part of more than a dozen acquisitions—empowering internal alignment, cultural integration, and clear, confident messaging during periods of change. In addition, Stacey helped firms activate alumni networks through digital marketing to generate referrals of both customers and candidates, extending brand equity well beyond current employees.

Stacey is the co-author of *Government Marketing Best Practices 2.0: What You Need to Know for Accelerated Success* and hosts the podcast *Branding the Beltway*. She lives in Fairfax, Virginia, with her husband, daughter, and their four rescued pets. Stacey holds a master's degree from Johns Hopkins University, a bachelor's degree from the Commonwealth University of Pennsylvania, and serves on the Board of Directors for Brain Injury Services of Northern Virginia.

Connect with Stacey:

Connect: https://www.linkedin.com/in/staceypiper/

Learn: https://piperstrategies.com/connection-quotient/

Listen: https://open.spotify.com/show/2NlHEzYbnzw9EQav9jSzh5

Subscribe: https://linkedin.com/newsletters/7061766992407527424/

CHAPTER 14

SHIFTING FROM "PERFECT FIT" TO "POTENTIAL CONTRIBUTOR"

BUILD A PEOPLE-FOCUSED CULTURE BASED ON TALENT ACQUISITION AND RETENTION

Aisha Scott, Founder and Chief Leadership Executive

MY STORY

The perfect candidate may have a perfect straight-line resume, but the best-fit candidate might have a curved road journey that actually amplifies their passion to be a potential contributor to your organization in the most insightful way.

Early in my career, I landed my dream job as a training instructor and professional coach. The position aligned with my personal values and allowed me to nurture and support the onboarding of newly hired employees by ensuring they had the tools to succeed in their position and careers. Although I loved my job as a trainer and performance improvement coach, I walked away from it because I thought my success in the position came too easily, and I didn't understand the concept of "find your passion." It wasn't until years later (working for a company I loved but a position that didn't align with my values), that I had the aha moment: *My passion for helping other people grow in their careers is what actually fills my cup.*

The self-reflective moment was refreshing, but the roadblock that appeared was that the company I worked for didn't have a designated HR Team. I swiftly searched for positions outside of the company to return to the people development side of Human Resources.

After applying for a number of positions without an offer, I received an unexpected "aha" moment when an auto-generated response informed me that not having my degree was the next roadblock in returning to the career where I was most passionate. While completing an online application, I came to a screen that asked five very simple questions regarding my professional skills. I was able to answer yes to four of the five questions, with the fifth question asking if I had a degree. Although I had completed 120 college credits and was three courses away from a dual Bachelors degree, I had taken a break from college due to burnout and life changes. Thus, my answer to the fifth question was "no," and I clicked the submit button. The very next screen popped up with bold red letters and stated, "Unfortunately, you do not qualify for this position." Yet another roadblock. I had taken a break from completing my bachelor's degree several years prior and knew that completing the final three classes would get me past this new roadblock. Unfortunately, due to being out of school for more than ten years, I was told by the college admissions representative, "You'll have to complete ten classes and not just three." This was yet another roadblock I had to overcome to return to my passion for HR and people development. After having a brief emotional moment and determined to reclaim my seat in the Human Resources space, I told the admissions counselor, "I will complete these ten classes over the next year." Her response to me was "you don't have to rush," but I knew this was just the next roadblock for me to overcome to advance in my journey. I enrolled in classes during the Fall 2015 semester and took two classes in the fall, two over winter break, two in the spring of 2016, one over the summer, and three the following fall to complete my degree program in December 2016. I took on all that while working full-time, traveling to the West Coast every other month for work, completing homework assignments at 8:59 pm PST on work trips to meet the 11:59 pm EST deadlines, and navigating the new role of being a single parent. I also knew that I had to show employers that my value-add was top-notch, so I paid out of pocket for additional professional certifications.

Soon after graduating with my Bachelor's degree in December 2016, I landed a job that allowed me to return to a position and career that aligned with my personal values, supporting and developing others while also creating and implementing policies to enhance the employee experience.

That moment refueled my focus to return to HR to equip leaders with the knowledge, tools, and strategies to develop staff to achieve company goals. For me, that path meant starting my own HR consulting company, becoming a certified life and executive coach, and attaining a master's degree in I/O psychology.

THE STRATEGY

Many organizations recruit with an external focus on hiring the *perfect candidate*; however, they often miss the mark in attracting and retaining quality applicants due to a lack of an internal focus on culture and onboarding. The two major areas where many companies and businesses fail regarding culture and onboarding include: (1) not preparing an effective recruitment and interview process to introduce and onboard applicants to the company, and (2) lacking a pre-defined new employee onboarding experience that incorporates structured training, career development, and culture immersion.

To start, how does an organization determine the *perfect candidate* for an open position? Is it the most qualified applicant, or the applicant that brings the most quality to the table? Before a hiring manager gets to the interview stage of looking for the *perfect candidate*, the company should evaluate if it has established an organizational culture and implemented onboarding programs prepared to advance the career of a potential contributor. In most cases, the probability of finding a qualified, perfect candidate is less than 20%. However, recent HR trends show that the probability of finding a quality potential contributor with adequate transferable skills is closer to 60-80%.

Success can be accomplished in two ways: (1) having a P.R.E.P. process to attract and interview applicants, and (2) having the onboarding and development T.O.O.L.S. to successfully implement the transition from applicant to new employee.

THE P.R.E.P. PROCESS TO ATTRACT AND INTERVIEW A POTENTIAL APPLICANT

- **P** – Preferred versus Required
- **R** – Real-Life Experiences
- **E** – Eliminate Bias
- **P** – Provide Next Steps

Before an applicant can apply for a position, the company has to send out a job posting. The job posting should be clear and succinct, present job titles and required duties that align with industry standards, and avoid an overwhelming list of job functions that would scare an applicant away.

Preferred vs. Required – Creating Effective Job Descriptions

Poorly written job descriptions may be contributing to low applicant responses or unqualified applicants. Many managers or employers treat the job posting or job description as a wish list of items for the perfect candidate; however, applicants typically will not complete the application if they cannot decipher between what is truly a required skill and what is just a preferred skill. Several organizations that compile data sourcing for HR related studies note that applicants are less inclined to apply for job opportunities with vague position-specific competencies, unclear success metrics, or over-inflated qualifications.

To create an effective job description, a company must determine the absolute required (or must-have) skills someone needs to complete the daily tasks of the job at a basic level of proficiency and how any preferred (or like-to-have) skills will play a role in advancing organizational impact. These are the baseline competencies for having a job description focused on attracting a qualified, perfect candidate versus creating a job description that could attract a quality, potential candidate.

- The required skills listed on the job description should be attainable. What are the very bare minimum knowledge, skills, and abilities (KSAs) that a person needs to have to complete the daily day-to-day functions of this position? This section of the job description should focus on the daily tasks that take place 70%-80% of the time.

- The preferred skills listed on the job description should be industry-specific and geared towards mid-level positions. This section should not be a barrier to applicants for entry-level positions. Remember, although there are some professional traits that are nice-to-haves, companies will still be required to train this new employee to complete the tasks based on company-specific policies and procedures.

Real Life Experiences – Interviewing For Potential Not Perfection

The actual interview isn't just an opportunity for the applicant to reiterate their resume, but rather for the hiring manager to learn about how the applicant's personal KSAs and professional experiences can add value to the open position. It's a good practice to create an interview template with specific behavioral interview questions based on the job description.

Behavioral interview questions should be structured in a way that won't generate a "yes" or "no" response from the applicant, but rather a response that showcases an example of a real-life experience they've encountered with a similar scenario. Behavioral interview questions typically start with prompts such as "tell me about a time when," "describe a moment when," or "share an experience where you." These types of questions allow the hiring manager to see in real-time how the applicant communicates, if they're a strategic thinker, and if they have any transferable skills from another position, company, or industry that can make them a potential contributor.

A good interviewer will be able to listen to the applicant's responses to the behavioral questions and pick up cues for any unconventional transferable skills that could add value to the actual position, department, or company. In moments when a candidate is still relatively new in their career, or they're changing industries, they might not have any industry-specific examples; however, they may have position-specific similarities (or transferable skills) that would make them a good fit as a potential contributor.

Eliminate Personal Bias – Interviewing With a Mask

During the interview process, it's important that hiring managers focus on how the applicants' KSAs and experiences align with the function of the job role and eliminate roadblocks to hiring based on their personal perspective. Removing personal biases during an interview can be tough at times because there is a very short window to ask all the pertinent questions, while your brain is quickly connecting the dots subconsciously, and the applicant is still in front of you. The core definition of the term bias is simply a preference. Some biases are defined as explicit (preferences/ attitudes an individual is consciously aware of) or implicit (preferences/ attitudes that impact decision making, that may be a subconscious response). When explicit biases impact hiring decisions, it can open the door for HR discrimination concerns. When implicit biases impact hiring decisions, it might mean missing out on a good potential contributor.

If the person made it to the interview stage, that means that something on their resume caught your attention. During the interview, hiring managers should stick to the behavioral questions template, actively listen to the applicant's actual responses related to their work experiences, focus on how their work history and experiences align with the required and preferred duties of the position, and eliminate trying to fill in the blanks about what aligns with you personally. Eliminating bias opens the door to bringing people to the company with fresh ideas and new perspectives.

Provide Next Steps in the Application Process – Communicating the Culture

When the interview is completed, it's important to be prepared with defined next steps to communicate to the applicant. This helps to keep the applicant informed in a competitive job market. The communication experience that the applicant has throughout their application process assists them with experiencing the company culture regarding communication, employee engagement, and organizational norms. Some applicants may choose not to move forward with a company if they see or feel that communication is lacking professionalism or engagement.

THE T.O.O.L.S. YOU HAVE IN PLACE TO ATTRACT, DEVELOP, AND RETAIN A HIGH-CALIBER EMPLOYEE

- **T** – Training Goals
- **O** – Orientation Programs
- **O** – Onboarding Plan
- **L** – Learning Plan
- **S** – Succession Plan

During the interview process, applicants show how much interest they're willing to invest in the company. Once the transition from applicant to employee occurs, it's now time for the company to show how it will invest in the new employee. Having T.O.O.L.S. in place to assist with the new employee's onboarding, allows them to feel seen, appreciated, and prepared.

Training Goals

Identify the basic knowledge, skills, and abilities (KSAs) an employee needs to be successful in this position and clearly define them on the job description (JD). Clearly defined KSAs and JDs provide a baseline for training goals focused on task-related expectations and will assist with coaching and accountability in the future.

Orientation Processes & Programs

Immerse the new employee into the company culture and educate them on company norms, policies, and behaviors. The orientation process may consist of a full-blown structured program, 1-on-1 interactions, or intermittent online learning modules. In either case, the initial orientation onboarding component will allow the new employee to learn about the company outside of just their department-specific tasks.

Onboarding Plan

Create a standardized roadmap to inform new employees about who, how, and when their position-specific training will occur. This template should align with the JD and specify the training methods (e.g., structured classroom training, 1-on-1 coaching, online training, third-party workshops). The onboarding plan is also a tool to assist current team members with building their leadership skills by assisting with training and coaching a new employee.

Learning Plan

Create an individualized roadmap to align with the employee's personal KSAs and the onboarding plan. The manager should meet one-on-one with the employee to evaluate their current strengths based on the JD and determine development needs to meet basic proficiency. This is also an opportunity for the manager to share designated timeframes or completion dates for the position-specific training. The learning plan will assist with establishing knowledge expectations and future-state performance management accountability.

Succession Plan

Succession planning is a critical component of not only organizational strategic planning, but also inter-departmental sustainability. Staff development is an integral component of a successful succession plan because it can assist companies and departments with ensuring that there is continuity with knowledge of business operations in the unexpected case that a key employee is unavailable. Implementing defined talent development strategies at the beginning of the hiring process forces leaders to put an emphasis on a long-term plan for who will be prepared to advance in the succession plan.

The last key part in defining the T.O.O.L.S. is to be aware of the different learning, communication, and leadership styles of a multi-generational workforce. A strategic focus on the multi-generational workforce is also a component of a strong succession plan. When new generations enter the workforce, it's imperative that leaders consider how the T.O.O.L.S. may need to shift to remain relevant and attract quality and qualified applicants. Effectively managing a multi-generational workforce requires companies to implement new trends to stay relevant (i.e., technology, benefits, systems, etc.) while also ensuring that individual contributors within the organization are still being given the opportunity to grow and develop when change occurs.

By incorporating all of the T.O.O.L.S., companies can ensure that they're not just setting their employees up to be successful in their roles, but also helping to ensure organizational sustainability, improving retention through empowerment and engagement, and reducing risk by decreasing single-point-of-failure occurrences.

Aisha Scott is the CEO of Time To Impact 365 Consulting and The Real Boss Ladies of Human Resources. She is a sought-after HR Consultant and Executive Coach, certified ICF Life Coach, inspirational and professional keynote speaker, college professor, and a mom.

Aisha Scott has over 20 years of professional experience and leadership expertise within the financial services, commercial real estate, and multi-family management industries. Aisha is a certified Training Instructor, ICF Life Coach, MBTI practitioner, and HR professional who holds a Master of Science degree in Psychology focused on Industrial/Organizational Development. She is an Executive Leadership Coach with Towson University's Dr. Nancy Gramick Leadership Institute and an adjunct faculty lecturer at the Community College of Baltimore County, where she focuses on continuing education programs related to HR policies, business management, and communication and leadership for government officials. Her passion for developing corporate professionals and her engaging facilitation style have placed her in front of organizations such as Georgetown University, Bank of America, the US Army Core of Engineers, the Maryland Police and Correctional Commission, the McCormick Company, the Department of Defense, and NOAA. She is also a member of the American Business Women's Association, the International Coaching Federation, a Board Member of ATD Maryland Chapter, and a former Board Member of the Greater Baltimore SHRM (formerly Chesapeake Human Resources Association), leading the Workforce Readiness committee.

Connect with Aisha:

Professional Website: www.AishaTheEducator.com

Business Website: www.TimeToImpact365.com
www.BossLadiesOfHR.com

YouTube: https://www.youtube.com/channel/UCrUiB45rMBMQ2gm6uyBbIgQ

LinkedIn: https://www.linkedin.com/in/aishascott/

TimeToImpact365: www.linkedin.com/company/timetoimpact365

Real Boss Ladies of HR: www.linkedin.com/company/therealbossladiesofhr

CHAPTER 15

BUILDING A CANDIDATE CENTRIC MODEL

HUMANIZING HIRING IN THE AGE OF AI

Sonia E. Pacheco, SHRM-SCP, PCC

MY STORY

FEBRUARY 25, 2019

All I could think was, *she does not look good. Her eyes and skin look very yellow.*

I drove home after a long, busy Monday at work. Houston, Texas, traffic was as usual, bumper-to-bumper, despite being past 6:00 p.m. I remember feeling accomplished, excited, and exhausted. Our HR team, which worked diligently for two years, has just launched a new Human

Capital Management (HCM) system. One week into our go-live, everything finally started to work as expected.

I was excited to get home and hug my young children, one and four years old at the time. I was also excited to share how my day went with my parents, who were living with us. My husband left earlier that morning for an international business trip, so I could share all the exciting project updates with my parents. They both love listening to all my work stories!

I remember feeling deeply grateful for the opportunity to manage it all. *How is this my life? This is an amazing once-in-a-lifetime project. My HR team is the best. I am working for a global company, and I'm still managing motherhood and marriage well. All of it is somehow mine, and all of it is a blessing.*

My husband felt the same way. We were especially grateful to my parents, whom we convinced four months earlier to relocate from the West Coast, and who moved in with us to help our growing family.

I'm home! I opened the door, took off my shoes, and walked straight to the kitchen.

Dinner was ready—my mom stood by the kitchen island, but something didn't seem right. I noticed her eyes and skin looked different. I wasn't sure if I was making things up or if my tired eyes were playing a trick on me. It was already dark outside, so I turned up the kitchen lights dimmer to be sure. The lighting was not an issue.

"Are you feeling okay?" I asked her. "I felt ill all day; the symptoms seem to be getting worse," she said. My dad nodded in agreement. "She spent most of the day lying down."

She was wearing a T-shirt and long pants, so I could clearly see her arms and face. Her complexion seemed yellowish.

We decided to go to urgent care for an evaluation. Upon arrival, they encouraged us to go directly to the emergency room, explaining, "Your mom will need additional testing. The urgent care has limitations."

I remember comforting her on our drive to the emergency room. "There's a brand-new medical facility in the neighborhood. They will take excellent care of you," I reassured her. I told her we'd get to the bottom of what was going on so she could finally find relief and comfort.

To our surprise, the emergency room had only a few people waiting, and my mom was checked in within an hour. While we waited in the exam room, I studied her complexion under the bright white lights. She was lying down, looking up at the ceiling. She seemed uncomfortable, anxious, yet chatty.

A nurse arrived wheeling in an ultrasound machine and began examining my mom's abdomen. It looked like my pregnancy ultrasound. After asking my mom a few questions and taking several images, she told us, "The doctor will be in shortly with an update." We both believed she would be evaluated and discharged that night.

With my husband traveling, my dad at home watching my two children, and me sitting in the emergency room with my mom, this assumption gave me comfort. It was close to 10 p.m., I felt drained, and I was scheduled for an early start the next morning. It was only Monday, and I was already exhausted.

There was a knock at the door, followed by the doctor's entrance and brief introduction. "We found a mass near your mom's liver and pancreas, about the size of a golf ball. She will need to be admitted for further testing."

My heart sank.

English was not my mother's first language, so I had to gather myself and carefully translate the news. She was admitted that night.

I texted my husband:

"I need you to come home; my mom was admitted to the hospital."

He was confused by the text message and the time of day, so he immediately called my cell phone. He had just left that morning, and everything seemed under control. "I'll take the first flight home," he said without hesitation.

FEBRUARY 26, 2019

I remember waking up thinking, *"This is all a bad dream."* Very soon, I realized this was now our new reality.

That morning, I called my boss and updated him on the situation. He knew we did not have family in the city—both of our families lived on the West Coast. He also knew I had become my parents' primary caregiver after my dad suffered a stroke that left the left side of his body impaired the year before, and he was in physical therapy treatments at that time.

His response was simple: "Take all the time you need and let us know how we can help. When you can, please share an update."

My boss, a man of faith, reassured me that he would keep my mom in his prayers, something that brought me great comfort. I felt fortunate to be a part of a wonderful company and a team that had become an extension of my family. I used to call them my "Texan family," something my boss and co-workers would jokingly tease me about: "Can you just call us your 'family'? Why do you have to say *Texan*?"

After my husband arrived home, my dad and I went to the hospital to check on my mom. The hospital staff was incredibly kind the night before, and although I couldn't stay overnight, I knew my mom was well cared for.

Her room felt new, modern, and very spacious. I felt proud that I could provide my mom with comfort during uncertain times. "Were you able to sleep?" I asked. She gently nodded. The room accommodated my dad's wheelchair and had a spacious bathroom and shower.

We waited a few hours for the doctor to come by. My mom was lying in bed; my dad sat beside her in his wheelchair, holding her hand. I sat on the other side of her feet and next to the doctor. We all felt optimistic and hoped to hear that she could be discharged.

"Further testing has revealed a mass in the head of the pancreas, about the size of a golf ball. The tumor is large and obstructs her bile duct, causing the yellowish color of her eyes and skin. This condition is called jaundice," the doctor explained.

Knowing my mother's limited English, he took out a pen and paper and began drawing the liver and pancreas, showing us exactly where the tumor was. He then reviewed lab results, explaining that tumor markers suggested a high possibility of cancer. Her condition was critical; biopsy and surgery were necessary to determine a diagnosis and an immediate treatment plan.

Although we did not have certainty that it was cancer, I felt the gravity of the situation. A few years earlier, I saw a poster about it in my primary care physician's office and read about it, thinking, *Gosh, pancreatic cancer diagnosis sounds more like a death sentence.* The five-year post-diagnosis survival rate was only 5%.

I immediately felt like I was punched in the gut. A knot formed in my throat, big and suffocating. I didn't know what to say or how to translate this in a way that would offer comfort. My body tensed up, and I felt anxiety for the first time with internal shaking. I crumbled—hugging my mom's legs, trying desperately to pull myself together, but failing to do so. I felt my mom and dad's hands rubbing my back.

I cried loudly like a young child. I couldn't stop. There I was—broken—being comforted by my parents while we all faced our biggest fear—potentially losing my mom and losing her quickly.

They didn't fully understand everything the doctor said, so once again, I searched for the right words and explained the situation to them.

MARCH 7, 2019

After further blood testing, a biopsy, and an emergency surgery, the diagnosis was confirmed: Stage IV pancreatic cancer.

We were in disbelief. *How and when did cancer develop to stage IV? This cannot be possible.* She had mild symptoms that progressed in just a week. I kept telling myself: *This is impossible. She would not hide this from me. She lives with me; she helped care for my dad and children.* Most importantly, no one in our large family had cancer. *This simply cannot be our new reality.*

In addition, my mother never drank, never smoked, never did drugs, was healthy, and was only 61 years old. The following day, my mother was discharged with a treatment plan and scheduled appointments to see a GI oncologist. Unfortunately, pancreatic cancer is often found late because early symptoms are subtle.

FEBRUARY 25, 2020

On February 25th, 2020, 365 days after diagnosis, I witnessed my mother take her last breath.

As an HR professional, I've always had a window into others' lives, the good, the not-so-good, and everything in between. In our profession, you learn to be resourceful and proactive, and you know you aren't alone when life gets tough. Now it was our family's turn to experience that side of life.

She fought hard to beat cancer, and never once did I hear her complain to anyone about anything or blame anyone for her diagnosis. She tried every chemotherapy, homeopathic, and every possible alternative treatment. She showed extraordinary strength and resilience through the most challenging times. Though she didn't want to die, the idea that she would meet God gave her peace and comfort, particularly when she experienced excruciating pain, which became a daily challenge to manage.

Being her caregiver and witnessing her daily struggles shaped my soul and revealed my purpose, providing me with a clear roadmap to how I should live my life: there's nothing more important in this world than your faith, family, friends, and letting people know you love them.

HER LEGACY IS MY PURPOSE

Her last year with us was filled with family, love, laughter, pain, and many goodbyes. Those who knew her described her as:

- A woman of deep faith in God.
- A devoted family member whose love knew no bounds.

- A woman of strong, unshakable values, quiet wisdom, and extraordinary strength.
- Exceptionally hardworking, yet funny and feisty, especially with my father, to whom she was married for 44 years.
- A beautiful human inside and out with radiating warmth and kindness. Her gentle smile and kind eyes brought peace to everyone she met.

Before her diagnosis, we talked about work every day. We had similar work schedules, and she was often the person I called during my commute home. She loved working, and we loved sharing the details of our days; it was one of the many ways we connected.

After her diagnosis, she never once spoke about work or any of her work experiences. I knew that the absence of work conversations carried profound meaning.

Since her passing, I've chosen to live differently, to be authentic, to deepen my faith, to love wholeheartedly, to live unapologetically (life is too short!), and to be a guiding light for others when they need it most.

My love for my career isn't about filling job vacancies; it's about honoring people and their journeys. Behind every job application is a human being carrying hope, responsibility, and the desire to contribute something meaningful to the world. By transforming hiring functions, I can touch thousands of lives at once and create dignity in moments that are often transactional and uncertain.

Coming from a large and hardworking family, I feel a deep responsibility to create and protect opportunities for others, to open doors, keep them open, and advocate for anyone who needs someone in their corner.

As we know, COVID-19 forever changed the hiring experience. Stories of impersonal processes, prolonged silence, and dehumanizing systems have left lasting impacts on people's confidence, morale, and livelihoods. Long before these challenges were amplified, and even more urgently now in the age of AI, I knew we needed a better way.

That's why I created the model you'll read about next. First developed in 2017 and applied across industries and organizations, it proves that transforming and humanizing hiring is not only possible but also powerful and rewarding.

THE TOOL

The Candidate Centric Model

A practical tool for humanizing hiring in the age of AI

Over the past two decades, I've studied thousands of organizations, reviewing their websites, mission statements, values, branding, job portals, and social media presence. Nearly all of them speak passionately about their people, customers, innovation, and culture.

Yet behind the scenes, most hiring experiences tell a different story.

Candidates encounter unclear processes, long delays, automated silence, and fragmented communication often at moments when they're most vulnerable. These gaps don't exist because leaders don't care. They exist because hiring is still treated as a support function instead of a strategic one.

This tool challenges that assumption.

The Candidate Centric Hiring Model is not a checklist. It's a repeatable system leaders can use to design, evaluate, and improve hiring functions with the same discipline they apply to revenue, operations, and customer experience.

The goal is simple:

Create hiring experiences that are efficient, compliant, data-informed, and deeply human at the same time.

You can use this tool to:

- Audit your current hiring approach
- Design or redesign hiring processes
- Pressure-test decisions before scaling automation or AI
- Align leaders, recruiters, and technology around a shared experience

What follows are the seven decisions that make the model work.

STEP 1: DESIGN A CLEAR HIRING STRATEGY

Decision: *What roles and experiences matter most to the business right now?*

Start by aligning hiring with business reality, not assumptions.

This means clearly identifying:

- Revenue-generating and mission-critical roles
- Near-term vs. future talent needs
- The kind of candidate experience you want to be known for

The output of this step is clarity:

A hiring strategy that supports growth, provides clarity to all stakeholders, and reflects where the business is actually headed, not where it hopes to be.

STEP 2: ESTABLISH STRONG TEAM LEADERSHIP

Decision: *Who owns the hiring experience, and how much authority do they have?*

Every hiring system needs a clear leader. This person must:

- Genuinely care about candidates, employees, and business goals
- Be willing to challenge outdated practices
- Advocate for the candidate experience across automation, messaging, and human touch points

This leader acts as a bridge, translating business needs into hiring priorities while keeping people at the center of decisions.

The output here is accountability:

Hiring stops being everyone's side job and becomes someone's responsibility.

STEP 3: EVALUATE YOUR EMPLOYEE VALUE PROPOSITION (EVP)

Decision: *Why should someone choose to work here, and does the candidate's experience match the message?*

Your EVP should answer one question clearly:

Why you, over another employer?

This step requires alignment across:

- Job postings
- Recruiter messaging
- Interviews
- Your website and social presence

The output is consistency:

What candidates hear, see, and experience should tell the same story, without exaggeration or disconnect.

STEP 4: KNOW YOUR BUSINESS THROUGH DATA AND ANALYTICS

Decision: *What is actually happening in our hiring system, and where are we guessing?*

Data brings discipline to hiring. Focus on metrics that inform decisions, such as:

- Time to fill
- Offer acceptance rates
- Cost per hire
- Turnover by role, business function, tenure, and reason

The output is insight:

You can identify pain points, risks, and opportunities before they become people problems.

STEP 5: EVALUATE TECHNOLOGY AND DESIGN CANDIDATE-CENTERED PROCESSES

Decision: *Is technology serving the experience, or replacing it?*

AI and automation should remove friction, not empathy and human connection.

In this step, assess:

- Where automation improves speed and clarity
- Where human connection still matters most
- Whether communication feels transparent and timely

Your hiring team is essential here. Involve them directly. They see what works and what breaks every day.

The output is flow:

A hiring journey that feels intentional, easy to navigate, and human at every touchpoint.

STEP 6: MANAGE BUDGET AND RESOURCES INTENTIONALLY

Decision: *Where will long-term investment create the greatest return?*

Instead of defaulting to placement fees, invest in:

- Scalable technology
- Process improvement
- Training for hiring leaders and your Recruiter(s)

Leverage job board partners and vendors as strategic allies, not transactional tools.

The output is sustainability:
Hiring becomes less reactive, more predictable, and easier to scale.

STEP 7: PRACTICE EFFECTIVE CHANGE MANAGEMENT

Decision: *How will we help people adopt this, not just understand it?*

New hiring approaches require new behaviors.

Train leaders and recruiters on:

- Interviewing with clarity and care
- Communicating transparently
- Using frameworks to stay aligned

No matter how automated your system becomes, there will always be a moment when a candidate meets your organization, virtually or in person.

This moment matters.

The output is confidence:

Leaders know how to show up, even in difficult or emotional conversations.

HOW TO USE THIS TOOL

Use the Candidate Centric Model:

- As an annual or quarterly audit
- Before implementing or updating AI-driven workflows and upgrading systems
- When hiring feels slow, impersonal, or misaligned

Hiring is one of the few business functions where technology and humanity must coexist. This model exists to ensure neither gets lost.

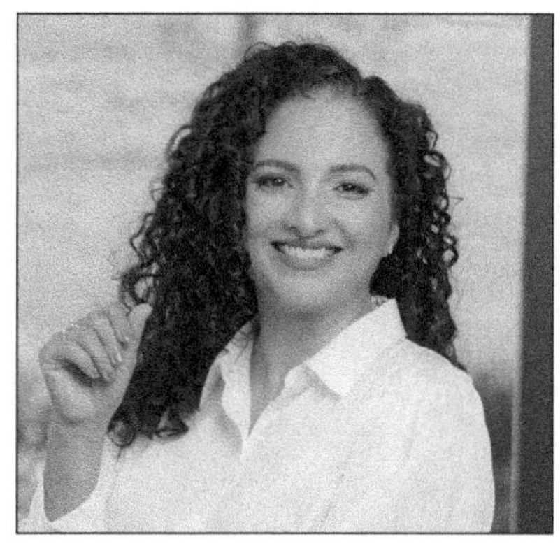

Sonia E. Pacheco, SHRM-SCP, PCC, is an expert in Talent Acquisition and Human Resources Management with a proven record of leading successful recruitment and talent acquisition initiatives for organizations ranging from small, family-owned businesses to large public corporations. She is known for connecting exceptional talent with meaningful, life-changing opportunities and building strong, high-performing teams that help businesses thrive.

In addition to her expertise in staffing and recruitment, Sonia is an experienced human resource professional, career coach, and talent consultant. She partners with both individuals and organizations to help them reach their full potential and achieve meaningful goals.

Sonia holds a Bachelor of Arts in Organizational Leadership from Chapman University and maintains several recognized Human Resources certifications. Her bilingual skills enable her to serve a diverse client base and deliver content in both English and Spanish.

Outside of her professional work, Sonia is a proud daughter, wife, mother, sister, aunt, and friend. She can often be found enthusiastically cheering on her children at their weekend soccer matches.

Connect with Sonia:

Website: https://talentbysp.com/

Email: spacheco@talentbysp.com

Career Coaching: https://talentbysp.com/contact/

Instagram: https://www.instagram.com/talentbysp/

LinkedIn: https://www.linkedin.com/in/soniapacheco/

CHAPTER 16

PEOPLE OVER PROCESSES

WHY CARING FOR YOUR EMPLOYEES FUELS BUSINESS SUCCESS

Katie L. Tanner, SPHR

MY STORY

It was the height of the COVID pandemic, and every phone call felt like it might break someone's heart.

I led an HR consulting team supporting skilled nursing facilities (SNFs) during the worst months of the pandemic. Patients were isolated from families, staff worked relentless shifts, and leadership made tough calls with incomplete information as laws changed daily. There was no playbook or time to weigh the human cost of every decision.

Our staff grieved patients, avoiding calls to family members, and showing up exhausted day after day because someone had to take care of these people. We had processes in place and followed protocols. Compliance metrics looked good on paper, but our people were breaking, and I didn't fully see it until someone complained about a broken microwave.

That's when it hit me. *When a crisis hits, your processes don't save you. Your people do.* And we were failing our people.

THE $40 DECISION

We recently took over management of a facility that looked perfect on paper. It was profitable with four-star ratings, solid patient satisfaction scores, above-market wages, comprehensive benefits, and generous paid time off. The administrator genuinely didn't understand why turnover was so high. He pointed to the compensation packages, benefits, and the clean facility, convinced he checked all the boxes we're taught to check in HR school.

So, my team did what we always do when the numbers don't match the story. We went to the floor and talked to actual employees, all 200 of them across three stories. Within the first few interviews, the pattern became obvious: one time clock, one break room, one microwave that barely worked.

Think about what that means in a nursing facility where everything runs on a tight schedule. Staff on the third floor spent ten minutes of their 30-minute break just getting to the time clock, then waited in line behind 20 other people trying to heat up lunch. This is a setting where if one shift runs five minutes late, the whole day cascades, and everyone's break gets pushed back. By the end of the shift, some employees finally got lunch at 4 PM after seven straight hours of patient care.

A microwave, I remember thinking. *This is the problem? We can fix this TODAY.*

I sat down with the administrator to debrief and went through everything we heard. When I got to the microwave issue, he actually rolled his eyes and said, "If I hear about that damn microwave one more time, I'm going to lose it."

"So, you already know about it?"

"It's all anyone talks about."

"Seems like an easy fix."

"It's not in the budget."

I stared at him. "A forty-dollar microwave isn't in the budget?"

"Every dollar I save impacts my bonus structure. This one works. No need to get another one."

And there it was, laid bare. This administrator genuinely believed he was doing right by his staff with competitive pay, good benefits, and a clean facility. But he prioritized his bonus over a basic quality-of-life issue affecting 200 employees every single day, not because he was a bad person, but because that's what his incentive structure rewarded. This is what we're up against in HR.

WHAT CHANGED

I went around him! I called our payroll team and ordered time clocks for every floor. I found storage rooms that were converted to break spaces with tables, and added microwaves on every floor that were installed the next day, with *two* in the main break room on the first level. You'd have thought we announced across-the-board raises based on the number of people smiling in the hallways and thanking my team and me personally for something that cost less than one hour of consultant time.

But here's what really changed. Within three weeks, voluntary turnover dropped as staff who were job-hunting put applications on hold. New hires stopped washing out in the first 90 days, employee referrals went up, and patient satisfaction scores got even better. None of that was because of a microwave. It was because staff finally felt like someone was listening, like someone saw them as human beings with legitimate needs rather than just labor costs to be managed. That shift in feeling changed everything.

I wish I could say this was the only time I've seen something like this, but it's not even close.

THE PATTERN I KEEP SEEING

I've been doing HR for a while now across different industries, facility types, and organizational sizes, and I see versions of this microwave story everywhere. The details change, but the pattern doesn't. We invest thousands in employee engagement surveys and then don't act on the feedback because it's "not in budget" or "not the right time." We implement open-door policies, then get defensive when people actually walk through the door. We lose our best people and conduct exit interviews when we should've been doing stay interviews all along, and we're so busy recruiting new talent that we don't notice our current talent updating their LinkedIn profiles during their lunch breaks.

Here's what I need you to hear: people aren't problems to be solved with better processes. They're human beings who need to feel seen, heard, and appreciated, and when they don't feel those things, no amount of competitive pay or fancy benefits will keep them engaged. The organizations that weather crises, adapt to change, and actually retain institutional knowledge are the ones where people feel genuinely cared for, where leadership doesn't just collect feedback but actually responds to it, and where someone's daily experience matters more than a line item in next quarter's budget.

This is what I mean when I talk about restoring the Human in HR. We've gotten so focused on systems and processes and compliance that we've forgotten we're dealing with actual people who have lives and families and bad days and chronic pain and sick kids and aging parents. People who deserve to be treated like people, not resources to be optimized.

THE TOOL

THREE THINGS EMPLOYEES *ACTUALLY* NEED

After working with hundreds of organizations, I boiled employee engagement down to three fundamentals. Get these right, and everything else gets easier as retention improves, performance goes up, and culture strengthens. Miss these, and you're just rearranging deck chairs while your ship takes on water.

1. SEEN

Employees need to be seen as complete human beings, not just their job function.

We all know people have lives outside work, but do we actually acknowledge that in how we lead? When someone's performance dips, is your first move to document it for a performance improvement plan, or do you pull them aside and ask what's really going on? Being seen means leaders know your name and actually use it, not just in formal settings but when they pass you in the hallway. It means your contributions get acknowledged when you do good, solid, everyday work, not just when you stay until midnight or land the huge account. It means when you're struggling, someone notices even if you're trying to hide it.

And this starts from the top. If you're a CEO, do you know the names of your front-line employees and their "why"? Why do they show up every day, and what matters to them? If you don't, how can you possibly lead them effectively?

WHAT THIS LOOKS LIKE:

- You know what's happening in your team members' lives without them having to announce it
- You notice when someone's off, even when they're doing a good job of hiding it
- You remember what matters to them outside of work
- You invest in their development even knowing they might eventually leave for a better opportunity

Try This: Schedule 15-minute check-ins with each direct report at least monthly, where you don't talk about projects or deadlines. Ask "How are you really doing?" and "What do you need from me?" then shut up and listen without trying to fix everything or jumping in with solutions. Sometimes people just need to be seen.

When someone tells you they're struggling, resist that immediate urge to problem-solve and try this instead: "Thank you for trusting me with this. What would be most helpful for you right now?" Let them tell you what they need. Maybe it's flex time for the next two weeks, maybe it's just knowing you see them, or maybe they don't even know yet and just needed to say it out loud to someone who cares.

For Remote Teams: Schedule 15-minute video "coffee chats" with cameras on and no work agenda. Notice communication shifts: someone going silent or messages becoming paragraphs. Make remote workers speak first in meetings. One client pays a home office stipend of $100 a month to each employee without having to turn in any receipts. The money can be spent however they want, and it's automatic.

2. HEARD

Employees need to know their voice matters and that speaking up won't get them labeled as difficult.

The broken microwave wasn't really about the microwave. It was about employees raising an issue for months and being completely ignored. When people feel like their feedback goes into a black hole and nobody's listening, they stop talking, and when they stop talking, you lose your early warning system. By the time a problem finally becomes visible to leadership, it's already done serious damage as morale is shot, productivity is down, and your best people have mentally checked out or already left because nobody was listening to begin with.

I see this all the time. An organization will lose someone great, and leadership is shocked: "We had no idea they were unhappy!" Really? Because I guarantee that person tried to tell someone multiple times. They just weren't heard.

WHAT THIS LOOKS LIKE:

- People can raise concerns without fear of retaliation, eye-rolling, or being labeled a complainer
- Leadership actually acts on feedback, or at a minimum, explains why they can't
- Ideas get real consideration, even the ones that don't get implemented
- When changes are coming that will affect people, they get a voice in the process before decisions are final

Try This: Create a feedback loop where, when an employee raises an issue, you acknowledge it within 24 hours (it can be as simple as "Got this, looking into it"). Then actually follow through. If you can fix it, fix it and let them know. If you can't, tell them why and what you can do instead, then follow up to show what happened.

Keep a tracking system where you write down every concern someone brings to you, along with the date, the issue, and your planned response. Review it every week. This keeps things from getting lost and shows your team you mean it when you say their voice matters.

For Remote Teams: Create a feedback board where remote employees post concerns. Acknowledge within 24 hours, update as you investigate, and close with results. Start meetings by asking remote participants to share first.

3. APPRECIATED

Employees need to feel their work matters, and they're valued beyond their productivity numbers.

This is not about pizza parties or employee-of-the-month plaques that nobody wants. It's about genuine recognition that what someone does matters and that they matter. The administrator who wouldn't buy a $40 microwave sent the clearest possible message: you're worth less to me than my bonus. That kills morale faster than any bad policy ever could.

WHAT THIS LOOKS LIKE:

- Thank-you's that are specific, not generic ("Thanks for staying late to finish the Johnson report" beats "good job" every single time)
- Investment in people's growth, even when it doesn't directly benefit their current role
- Flexibility when life happens, because people have lives, and sometimes those lives are messy
- Compensation that actually reflects someone's value, not just whatever you can get away with paying

Try This: Keep a gratitude journal for your team where each week you write down three specific things team members did that made a difference. Then share those observations with them directly, not in their annual review but in the moment or close to it. "I noticed you stayed late to help the new hire set up. That made their first week so much better and showed them what kind of team we are."

Better yet, handwrite a thank-you note once a month using those gratitude journal entries. Take five minutes and actually write it out by hand. This is what I mean by restoring the Human in HR. In a world of automated everything, a handwritten note saying "I see you, I appreciate you, here's specifically why" is powerful because it reminds people that there's an actual human on the other end of all these policies and processes who cares.

And create ways for people to appreciate each other through a Slack channel for shout-outs or a few minutes at team meetings for people to recognize each other. When appreciation becomes multidirectional instead of just top-down, it becomes part of who you are as an organization.

For Remote Teams: Send recognition in public channels. Mail handwritten notes monthly with specific callouts. Send a gift card for lunch delivery occasionally. Acknowledge their time zone: "I know it's 7 am where you are, Bob. Thank you for making a call earlier to accommodate a client."

THE MICROWAVE PRINCIPLE

Every organization has a microwave story, some small fixable thing that leadership keeps ignoring: a broken coffee maker, uncomfortable chairs in the break room, parking assignments that make zero sense, or software that crashes three times a day while "IT is working on it." The size of the problem doesn't matter. What matters is what ignoring it says to your people: Your comfort doesn't matter here, your needs aren't important, you don't matter.

Here's the principle: **Fix the small things that matter to your people, and they'll take care of the big things that matter to your business.** If your people are thriving, your business is thriving. It's really that simple.

This doesn't mean you need unlimited resources or have to be perfect. It means paying attention, taking concerns seriously, and taking action when you can. Sometimes that action is fixing the problem. Sometimes it's explaining why you can't fix it right now, but here's what you can do instead. Sometimes it's just saying, "Yeah, I know this is frustrating. I see it too." When your people bring you their microwaves, they're really asking: "Do you see me? Do you hear me? Do you care?" How you answer those questions determines everything about your culture.

WHAT THIS MEANS FOR YOU

Processes matter, systems have value, and efficiency is important. I'm not saying throw all that out. But none of it works without people who actually care enough to make it work, and people only care when they feel cared for. You can't automate genuine appreciation, or systematize actually seeing someone, or create a process that makes people feel heard. These things take intention, attention, and the daily choice to put people first, even when it's inconvenient, even when it costs money, and even when it means someone's bonus might be a little smaller.

The organizations that make it through a crisis, adapt when everything changes, and actually keep their best people are the ones where leadership gets this. Where people feel genuinely cared for, where feedback gets action instead of being filed away, and where your daily experience matters more than next quarter's numbers.

This is about restoring the Human in HR and remembering that behind every badge number, every full-time employee, and every "resource" in your HRIS is an actual person. Someone's mom, dad, sibling, auntie, dog mom, or best friend. Someone who deserves to be treated like they matter, because they do.

When you serve your people well, really serve them, they'll go to extraordinary lengths for your organization, for your customers, and for each other, not because they have to but because they want to. It starts with something as simple as a microwave, or a conversation where you actually listen, or noticing that someone needs to be seen.

So, I'll ask you: What's the microwave in your organization? What's the thing your people keep bringing up that you keep putting off? What would it cost to fix it, not in dollars, but what would it cost to keep ignoring it?

What will you do today? How can you "BE THE REASON" your team feels seen, heard, and valued?

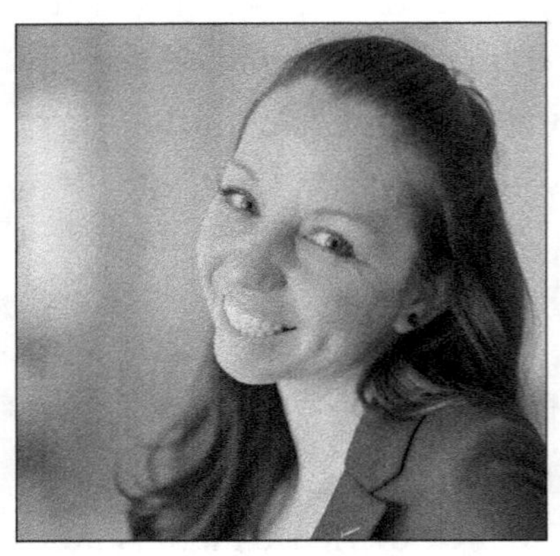

Katie L. Tanner, SPHR, is the Owner and President of KT HR Innovations, a fractional HR consulting firm specializing in restoring the Human in HR through people-centric practices. A founding member of the "Be The Reason" HR community, Katie has spent over a decade working with organizations across multiple industries and states to build workplaces where people feel valued and empowered.

With expertise in Health Care Compliance, Labor Relations, Union Shops, and multi-state employment law, including California, Katie provides strategic HR guidance to employers navigating complex workforce challenges. Her practice encompasses employee handbook development, policy creation, complex employee relations, internal investigations, union labor relations, collective bargaining, and merger and acquisition support.

Katie's philosophy centers on a fundamental belief: people are not problems to be solved with better processes. They are human beings who deserve to feel seen, heard, and appreciated. This approach has guided her work with organizations ranging from healthcare facilities to tech companies, helping leaders understand that investing in their people is the most important decision they can make.

As a trusted advisor to business owners and leadership teams, Katie works to streamline operations while maintaining a focus on people-centric processes that drive real results. Her work has helped countless organizations improve retention, strengthen culture, and build teams that go above and beyond—not because they have to, but because they want to.

When she's not consulting on HR shenanigans, Katie enjoys watching Padres baseball, eating sushi, drinking Cherry Coke, all things Harry Potter, planning the next house or yard project, and spending time with her husband and their Rottweiler/German Shepherd puppy, Jackie.

Connect with Katie:

Website: www.kt-hr.com

Email: katie.tanner@kt-hr.com

LinkedIn: https://www.linkedin.com/in/katielynntanner/

Facebook: https://facebook.com/kthrinnovations

CHAPTER 17

CULTURE KILLERS

HOW TO SAVE YOUR BOTTOM LINE

Emily Owens Channell

MY STORY

This can't be real.

"He's dead."

"What do you mean he's dead?"

"He's gone. He's gone. Em, your dad is gone."

I come off mute. I'm leading a virtual call with my team discussing the usual sales, staffing, and business priorities. It was a routine Wednesday morning in July, or so I thought.

"Guys, I don't know how to say this, but my dad just died. I have to go. Can you keep the call running?"

"Of course, anything you need. Keep us posted on how we can help." My team was nothing short of amazing. I wouldn't have wanted to be on any other call but with them.

CALL ONE.

"Calvin, my dad just died. My mom just called me. I've got to go figure a couple of things out; can you hold down the fort?"

I was shaking.

"My God, of course, go. Is there anyone you need me to call for you? We got this here, just go take care of what you need to."

"I'll make a call to my boss. Can you loop the rest of the group leaders in?"

I knew I could count on my district partner. We were running one of the hardest regions together, and I trusted him fully.

CALL TWO.

"Sis, did Mom call you?"

"Yes," she said, sobbing, hardly getting words out.

"We're leaving right now. Are you on your way?"

"Yes, we're almost there."

"Don't move the body until I get there. Don't let them take him." I was numb and couldn't picture what I was about to come home to, but I knew I needed to see him to believe it.

CALL THREE.

"Boss, my dad just died. I have to go home and help with arrangements. I probably need a week to figure this all out."

"Thank you for letting me know. Let me know if there's anything you need. Emily, I'm sorry for your loss."

The word started to spread. I probably made at least one hundred more calls that day, notifying friends and family while my mom, sister, and I were in shambles. And over the next few days, I received what seemed like one hundred more texts of shock, sympathy, and support. It was one text, only one day later, however, that burned in my memory.

"Did you see that email? Are you handling it?"

It was a text from my boss. My gut sank.

It had only been a day since my dad passed, and we had just talked on the phone the day before. I wasn't sure what I felt—angry, hurt, anxious, maybe a combination of them all—but it was clear the business and the machine that it was, was more of a priority than me. Looking back, that was the day I knew the company I poured my heart and soul into for years, the company I grew up in and cut my teeth in large leadership roles for, no longer had the culture I was aligned with.

Over the course of the next week, my busy team of twenty-six leaders, leading over five thousand employees, along with group leaders all over the region, showed up in so many ways for me. They came to the funeral, sent me flowers, wrote heartfelt notes of encouragement for my family, and sent me meals. They called to check up on me and even visited my dad's gravesite when the grave marker was finally done, just because they were in the area and figured they'd check on him for me.

It's crazy how long those markers take to make when death is sudden, as if the universe doesn't let you move on from the grief.

All of the support from an incredible team is unforgettable. But, equally unforgettable, is when your boss doesn't show up in the same way. When you have one manager leading the team who isn't necessarily a bad leader, but isn't a people-forward leader, it kills your culture.

It was from this experience that I knew I never wanted to be a leader who didn't lead by putting people first. And through the many more years of building teams, processes, and strong cultures, I realized these are the top five things that kill your culture.

THE TOOL

THE CULTURE AUDIT

NUMBER 1: THE BAD MANAGER

The Cost: High turnover.

Imagine this: your all-star employee, who is irreplaceable, asks, "Do you have time to chat today?" You welcome the engagement and are eager to schedule some time together, thinking:

I wonder what amazing deal they'll bring in for us. Or maybe they want to bring me up to speed on that project since I'll be out on vacation next week. Bahamas here we come.

They always keep everything on track. I don't know what I would do without them.

You willingly block time to talk, and when your meeting time finally approaches, they smack you with this,

"I'm handing in my resignation."

You frantically go through all of the questions: Why are you leaving? Where are you going? What will you be doing? Are you leaving for more money?

You find yourself circling back to why again and again. Their answer isn't good enough; you're not entirely sure why they're leaving, but you have a gut feeling. *I bet it's their manager.* You stay up until 3 am, continuing to question yourself and what you could've done differently to prevent this, how you didn't see this coming, and: *Oh crap, I guess that means canceling my trip to the Bahamas.*

The bottom line is that having bad managers on your team is hurting your actual bottom line. Not only is it costly to lose your all-star player, but you now have to invest in recruiting and training their backfill, which could take months of time, money, and effort. It's painful. Worse yet, you let the bad manager persist, and you have two more employees jump ship. You're in the hole, the department is stretched thin, customer satisfaction is slipping, and you're hanging by a thread. It's the perfect recipe for rushing into hiring the wrong backfill.

Sound familiar? We've all been there, and if you haven't, keep doing what you're doing. For the rest of us, here are ways to identify bad managers in your company.

1. Your managers aren't stepping up as coaches. You don't hear your managers coaching their team in real time, addressing problems, and training them to be better. Instead, you see their door closed. Good managers give up the star quarterback role and trade in their skills to be a winning coach.

2. They're talking only about processes and never about their people. They seem out of touch with their team, know nothing personal about what's going on in their team's lives, and they don't know their team has a silent text chain or Slack chain going on behind their back.

3. Problems roll up to you. People on their team seem to have a high frequency of concerns, questions, or performance issues. You feel like you're constantly solving your manager's problems for them.

What's the solution if you identify that you have bad management practices in your company? All companies should have a leadership development strategy, no matter the size or budget. It doesn't mean spending a lot on fancy training programs, but if you're going to have managers on your team, you need to equip them with tools to sharpen their leadership skills; tools like Tidewater HR Advisory provides to assess and deliver leadership principles.

NUMBER 2: THE BAD HIRE

The Cost: Lost revenue and client dissatisfaction

It's 5:30 pm on a Friday. You're exhausted from the work week, losing your all-star employee, and not to mention running to evening networking events, kids' extracurricular sports activities, parent-teacher meetings, you name it. You realize you didn't plan anything for dinner and have two hungry kids at home and a spouse to feed. You stop at your local grocery store on the way home for convenience. Your goal is to get in, get out, and pick up a quick dinner you can make in 20 mins or less. You grab a shopping cart, and as you walk in through the automatic doors, your head's racing and your stomach rumbles. The produce section is first. You see some fruit on sale and add it to your cart. You don't need it for dinner, but *I'll eat it this weekend, and besides, it's on sale.*

Then you throw some salad kits into your cart. You only need one, but *you never know which will be the crowd pleaser.* As you pass through the meat section, you try to decide between steaks or the buy-one-get-one chicken deal. *Who cares. I'm in a hurry. I'll get them both!*

You quickly find a few more things that you don't really need for your twenty-minute dinner prep, but are on sale. *Who can refuse a deal?* Heading toward the checkout line, you pass the baked good section, and since it's Friday, you justify adding a pack of freshly baked cookies to the mix. Before you know it, your cart's full, and suddenly, a quick dinner turned into items you didn't need. When you go to the grocery store hungry and in a hurry, you end up with a full cart of items you didn't need while paying three times more than what you planned.

The same is true with hiring. When you go to the grocery store hungry, you can end up with a bad hire, and when you have a bad hire, it's a sure-fire way to kill culture. A bad hire becomes pretty easy to spot. They seem great from the interview, but a few weeks in, you start to question their decisions, what they're doing with their time, and it becomes apparently clear that they don't fit the culture. You spend the time and money training them, assign them clients to service, and all of a sudden, they drop the ball. You have client complaints, employees complaining about picking up their slack, and you are on the verge of dropping or have already dropped clients, leaving money on the table.

The best way to mitigate a bad hire is to hire right the first time and to evaluate regularly how they're working out. Be involved early and often so you don't let months go by before realizing you made a giant mistake while looking at your customer satisfaction scores. Build your interview processes proactively and align them with your company values to ensure you hire right the first time.

NUMBER 3: KEEPING ENERGY SUCKERS ON BOARD

The Cost: Lost productivity and high turnover

Keeping energy suckers on board is a silent but deadly culture killer. We all have people in our lives who could be categorized as an "energy sucker." Maybe it's a friend, family member, or neighbor. Whoever it is, we all know at least one person that we've crossed paths with who seems to be miserable. What makes them miserable? They're most likely always blaming someone, complaining about something, or being defensive about their behavior. Now imagine working with that miserable person. Maybe it's a peer, a boss, or a senior leader. At all levels, that behavior is toxic and is one of the quickest but quietest ways to kill culture. That person doesn't work towards a solution; they spin their wheels, complaining about it. That person is not open to feedback; they spend their energy defending their position or blaming others. That person finds ways to complain about their coworkers instead of communicating and working together. Not only does this kill positivity and momentum in the workplace, but it's the biggest turnoff for high-performing team members who strive for excellence. If you want to be the best place to work in your industry and attract top talent, you can't have a culture of blaming and complaining. We've all heard the sayings "mediocrity breeds mediocrity" and "misery loves company."

Simply put, don't keep the energy suckers on board. Take inventory of who is currently an energy sucker. Help them get on board or get them off board.

NUMBER 4: FAILURE TO COMMUNICATE

The Cost: Productivity

I am fully convinced that every disagreement is a result of failed communication.

Communication is verbal and nonverbal. As a leader, you're communicating from the moment you walk through the door to the moment you leave for the day. How you greet and acknowledge others, interact in meetings, and keep your office door open or shut is all a form of communication that creates an impression on those around you. The micro and macro elements of communication are equally important.

The micro elements of communication are how you show up consistently and deliberately in interactions and control how you make someone feel. Have you ever talked with someone who you knew was half-listening? Perhaps you were trying to communicate something important, but they were looking down at their phone the whole time or typing on their computer screen without acknowledging you. Maybe their arms were crossed, or they walked past you in the morning without acknowledging you with a good morning greeting. You may not think these micro elements of communication kill culture, but they do.

I consider macro elements of communication to be the headlines you communicate to your team and across the organization. Some examples of these headlines could be company vision, someone new joining the team, or customer challenges to solve. Have you been part of a team where you didn't know what was going on? Maybe your boss didn't share key priorities with you. Maybe a coworker didn't communicate that someone was starting tomorrow, and now it's almost the end of the day, and you're playing from behind. No one likes to feel out of the loop. Even more importantly, when there is a breakdown in communication, the work doesn't get done, or it gets done twice by multiple people, only multiplying frustration. Culture suffers when there's a lack of communication across departments and when leaders do not communicate what's happening across the company. Here's why. Everyone wants to feel valued and respected.

Imagine this scenario. You have to decide between joining two companies.

Company 1: This company has a clear vision. Leadership teams, down to all levels, articulate where the company is headed and share both short and long-term goals. Every year, they communicate clear annual goals with milestones. When things get hard, they communicate the good and the bad. They have productive meetings that occur within departments where employees can share their priorities and what roadblocks they face. The leadership team models an open-door policy and is available for questions. People in the office are welcoming and acknowledge each other often.

Company 2: This company has a clear vision, but only the senior leaders know it. The team rarely hears from leadership or sees them in person. Even their direct manager doesn't model an open-door culture. They often keep their door closed, and when working remotely, they're hard to reach and not responsive. Meetings that are held are scheduled at the last minute and don't focus on a specific purpose. When things get hard, the company stays quiet about its position, leaving the team with many open questions.

Which company would you choose? Where would you feel more valued?

Improving communication is a challenging balance. If you have too little communication, your culture can feel disjointed and disconnected. If you over-communicate, your culture could feel micromanaged. If your communication seems off balance, start by adding this one simple question to the end of every meeting: "What do I need to share with my team and others?"

NUMBER 5: LACK OF INNOVATION AND AUTONOMY

The Cost: Revenue opportunities and overhead cost savings

Healthy cultures foster innovation and autonomy; in fact, they're essential for survival. Innovation in every industry looks different, but every employee at every level should be empowered to do their job and find ways to make it better. Decisions are often best made closest to the source. Think of it this way. You have a job role for a reason, and you hired the perfect person to fill it. The worst thing you can do to disengage that person immediately is to prevent them from reaching their full potential. Managers often avoid hearing new ideas for a variety of reasons. Maybe they don't think they can get new ideas approved; they get overwhelmed and don't know where to go with them, or they want it their way or the highway. But that lack of autonomy just kills culture and keeps senior leaders working on overdrive, all because they can't relinquish the reins to the team they have in place.

The idea for Amazon Prime Membership originated with an employee, Charlie Ward, who submitted it to an internal employee suggestion box to offer exclusive, fast shipping as part of an annual membership.

In 1977, Dick Brams, a regional manager, recognized that a meal designed for children could improve the dining experience. He pitched his idea for a boxed meal concept, which became the McDonald's staple, the Happy Meal.

Without innovation and autonomy, you're missing out on serious lost revenue opportunities and cost savings you didn't even know existed. You could have the next Happy Meal or Prime idea sitting right under your nose.

You might have some or all of these culture killers in your organization. If you do, don't panic. The good news is that you are now on your way to knowing where to attack what's killing your culture.

After more than a decade in Human Resources, **Emily Owens Channell** has seen what happens when businesses outgrow their HR systems before they even realize it. What starts as a few simple questions like, "How do we hire the right people?" or "How do I handle this employee issue?" quickly turns into the realization that the business needs a real HR strategy to keep growing.

I've built HR departments from the ground up for scaling organizations and supported leaders through those "what do I do now?" moments that every business owner faces. Along the way, I found myself becoming the person business leaders in my network called when they didn't know where to start. And in my own experience searching for and working with countless HR services, recruiters, and leadership resources, I found a lot of generic advice, but not enough care, urgency, or strategic depth.

That's why I founded Tidewater HR Advisory *to be the trusted partner leaders can call when they hit those inevitable HR moments and need clear, practical guidance.*

Tidewater HR Advisory gives small and mid-size businesses (and HR teams ready to scale) access to thoughtful, high-impact HR guidance without the cost of the corporate HR department. My approach is grounded in partnership and purpose: understanding your business, your people, and your goals, so together we can build the systems, leaders, and culture that help you grow and thrive. Visit tidewaterhr.com to learn more.

I'm grateful you're here, and I look forward to helping you grow your business where your people and performance thrive together.

- **Emily**

Connect with Emily:

Email: emily@tidewaterhr.com

Website: http://tidewaterhr.com

LinkedIn: https://www.linkedin.com/in/emily-owens-channell-mba/

WHAT YOU'RE
REALLY BUILDING

LEADERSHIP, LEGACY, AND LONG-TERM IMPACT

CHAPTER 18

FROM FIGHTING FIRES TO A STRONG FOUNDATION

A LEADERSHIP MODEL FOR CONSISTENCY, COMMUNITY, AND TRUST

Shelly Schoff

MY STORY

"We're going to need more help today."

It was one of those mornings—two call-outs before 7 a.m., a client complaint already waiting in our inbox, and a new trainee who wasn't ready to be on her own after 90 days of training.

For years, that text would've sent my entire day into an out-of-control spiral. I would cancel meetings, reshuffle the schedule, jump in and cover the phones, calm a frustrated client, coach a trainee, and quietly absorb whatever pressure came along with the chaos. I knew how to do it efficiently. I lived this day hundreds of times already. And most days, the business kept moving because I did.

But that morning, I didn't jump in.

Not because the situation wasn't critical, or the new trainee wasn't important, but because the business was no longer built to depend on me being the emergency backup system. We finally built consistency into our operations. We built a community within our teams. And we built trust in our leadership team.

The day wasn't perfect, and difficult decisions had to be made, but the company didn't fall apart without me.

That was the morning I realized I finally stopped being the only support structure holding everything together.

In the early days of building a business, firefighting feels not only necessary but also the only responsible thing to do. When everyone is counting on you, with few systems in place, limited layers of leadership, and constant unpredictability, stepping in is often the fastest, most immediate response. I solved problems quickly because I was closest to everything. I knew the clients, the quality standards, the expectations, and the people.

And if I'm being honest, there's an emotional reward in that role.

Putting out the fires made me feel indispensable. It created momentum, urgency, and a sense of purpose. When stepping in to fix things, the immediate relief is real, and that relief can become addictive.

But slowly, almost imperceptibly, constantly putting out fires becomes less about solving problems and more of an obstacle to growth and a distraction from your goals.

I didn't notice it at first. I only noticed that the same issues kept resurfacing. The same scheduling challenges. The same quality concerns. The same team members were asking for help making decisions, even though they were more than capable of making them on their own. The business wasn't failing, but it certainly wasn't thriving or becoming a stronger organization either.

It was barely hanging on, like a building with a fire smoldering just below the surface. No visible damage from the outside, but still at critical risk of crumbling at any minute.

The cost of running your business this way doesn't show up on a spreadsheet; it shows up in patterns—great hires that don't make it through training, repeated mistakes made due to poor communication, and constant bottlenecks that create frustration and disappointment.

When leaders constantly jump in to solve the problems, their teams learn to wait. When every answer comes from the top, ownership and accountability never fully take root in the employees. When systems rely on a single person's decision-making or availability, this bottleneck undermines consistency across the organization and slows growth and development.

I also began to notice the personal cost. I lived in "work mode," constantly distracted by whatever fire raged in the business in that moment. Even when I was physically present with my friends and family, I was mentally tethered to the business. In moments spent with my three precious grandsons, I tried to "send one quick text," leaving a constant feeling of guilt and disappointment in myself. *Why can't I just put down the phone and be here for them without distraction?* Time away from the business came with increased anxiety rather than rest.

Making plans for growth or dreaming big felt dangerous because it meant more moving parts, more potential fires, and more distractions from my life outside of the business.

Despite my best intentions, I wasn't truly leading. I held the business upright by force of will, believing my effort alone was enough while flames quietly gathered around me. And anything held up by a single support is always one moment away from collapse.

What finally shifted my thinking wasn't burnout; it was clarity.

I finally realized that so much of what I called support and commitment was actually control. I believed that stepping in and taking over was an act of kindness, and in many cases, it was. But over time, that care prevented others from developing confidence, judgment, and resilience.

Leadership, I learned, isn't about being the best problem-solver in the room. It's about building a team in an environment where problems can be solved without you. As a mom and a grandma, it finally connected: *By not allowing my team to be more involved in the problem-solving, I don't allow them to learn how to be the best versions of themselves and mature into the leaders they have the potential to become.*

That realization was uncomfortable. Letting go always is. But it was also freeing.

My transition away from firefighting didn't begin with absence. It began with intention—an intention to build smaller teams that anchored our crews together and created accountability, camaraderie, and support. These small teams, which we call PODs, have become a cornerstone of our leadership structure.

We focused first on consistency—not excellence, expansion, or optimization—just consistency. Clear expectations. Repeatable processes. Defined roles. Standards that lived outside of my head that could be easily followed without constant intervention and correction.

Consistency reduced chaos and made outcomes more predictable. And predictability created confidence, and our crews began to work together more efficiently.

From there, we leaned into our team's individual strengths and assigned ownership based on what people already did well. Decisions that once came directly to me were intentionally redirected to trained leaders in the field with clear guidelines for when escalation was necessary. Instead of waiting for answers, teams can troubleshoot issues together using shared standards and checks and balances to build a community with clear ownership of roles and responsibilities. Leaders in the field provide direct, immediate feedback, so coaching unfolds in the moment rather than days later. Relationships are built through shared responsibility and a common goal with a clear understanding of what success looks like.

People didn't just show up to work; they showed up for each other.

Slowly, trust evolved from something uncomfortable and awkward to something the organization practiced every day. Our POD Leads host monthly meetings where members are encouraged to ask questions, talk through concerns, and work together to resolve issues they experience in the field.

I learned that trust doesn't happen overnight. It's measured and grows when people feel supported, trained, and given permission to make decisions (and mistakes). Trust is strengthened when mistakes are treated as feedback rather than failure.

That morning, when the frantic text came in from my crew asking for help, every instinct in me knew how to respond. But this new leadership philosophy required restraint. It required allowing our systems to function the way they were designed, allowing the team to adapt as they were trained, and allowing the day to unfold without my intervention. Not because I didn't care, but because I finally cared more about the longevity of our business than the immediate gratification of putting out one more fire.

Not every day goes smoothly. Difficult conversations happen. Adjustments must be made. But the business stands strong, and our team has become the foundation of our organization.

And that's when I understood the difference between being an essential part of the daily operations and being an effective leader.

Fighting fires taught me how to respond. Building a strong foundation taught me how to lead. This distinction gave me the strength to withstand the heat of the fire, even as I stepped back and allowed someone else put out the flames.

That realization didn't come from a boardroom meeting or one specific training event. It came on an ordinary, chaotic morning, through a simple choice not to step in—and the quiet discovery that with proper planning and training, the structure of our organization and the resilience of our team could withstand the heat of the fire with or without me.

THE TOOL

FIREFIGHTING →FOUNDATION ROADMAP

Most leaders don't get stuck in firefighting mode because they lack vision or skill. They get stuck because they're capable, committed, and responsive. Those traits build businesses, but without structure, they can also trap leaders in an exhausting loop.

Firefighting persists because it works in the short term—problems get solved, clients stay happy, the day moves forward. But over time, the same issues return because the underlying system and the business's structure aren't solid.

Many leaders don't recognize this pattern until they try to step away for an extended time and realize how much of the business depends on them.

The purpose of the **Firefighting →Foundation Roadmap** isn't to assign blame or demand immediate change. Its main goal is to create awareness. A clear understanding of the issues within the organization is the first step toward creating a sustainable solution.

STEP 1: SEEING THE FIRES CLEARLY

The first step of this roadmap is to identify all recurring fires, not problems that are one-time disruptions, but the repetitive problems that return to continue to demand time and attention.

These patterns often point to a lack of clarity and underdeveloped role definitions rather than poor performance. For example, recurring missed deadlines may signal unclear ownership of a particular role.

Quality concerns may reflect inconsistent standards or training. Decision bottlenecks often reveal that authority hasn't been clearly communicated.

Calling out these fires isn't an admission of failure; it's an act of leadership.

STEP 2: UNDERSTANDING WHAT HOLDS THE BUSINESS TOGETHER

Next step, examine what currently holds each part of the business together. For each of the fires identified in step one, explain step by step how you'd personally handle that situation as if it were happening in the current moment.

Take a few moments to consider the following questions:

- Is there anyone else within your organization (besides you) who could follow these steps without missing a single step?
- Are these steps already documented?
- If someone needs to follow these instructions without supervision, what areas are they most likely to miss or struggle with?
- Are there **at least** two people within the organization who could complete this task successfully?

This step is often the most revealing. Many leaders discover that, while the business appears stable, it relies on informal knowledge and constant oversight from a few key individuals. That realization can be uncomfortable—but it's also empowering. You can't strengthen what you haven't seen clearly.

STEP 3: BUILDING COMMUNITY THROUGH OWNERSHIP

The third section focuses on communities built not just as culture alone, but as structure.

Consider where responsibility could move closer to the actual work itself for each of the fires identified in step 1. Who already demonstrates leadership without any title or authority? Where could clearer ownership reduce confusion and increase confidence? How would you accomplish this task today if you weren't available to complete the task yourself?

Community forms when people know what they own and trust that others are carrying their part. It doesn't eliminate problems, but it ensures they're addressed in advance through preparation rather than escalated in the moment.

STEP 4: EXTENDING TRUST INTENTIONALLY

Trust is often the hardest shift. Letting go can feel a little risky. But the tool reframes trust as a leadership skill rather than a personality trait.

Identify one responsibility you're ready to release from the fires listed in step one, and develop a structured training system for passing that one responsibility. Don't allow yourself to be overwhelmed by the whole role or the entire job description, but just this one individual task.

Think about the steps to accomplish this task and consider what it would look like to repeatedly train someone for this task, and think about how you'd want them to learn this information if you couldn't be present to assist. Would you want them to read your step-by-step instructions? Watch a video? Receive in-person training completed by someone else within the organization? Whatever the answer is, start developing that tool.

Once the tool is complete, consider the support and measurement systems you can put in place to help you feel more confident in assigning this task to someone else. What data or feedback would you need to feel confident that the task is being completed consistently? How frequently would you need to receive this information? Daily, weekly, monthly? What tool can you use in design to make it easy for that person to share that information with you? An email template? An end-of-day text? A screenshot? A Google Form, Sheet, or Document? Keep it simple and easy to digest so that, even on busy days, you have time to review and assess the results.

Trust grows through preparation, not abandonment.

BABY STEPS TOWARD FOUNDATION

Choose one single, intentional action to take—not a full transformation, not a perfect system—just one step toward greater consistency, shared ownership, or reduced dependence on a single individual.

Foundations aren't built overnight. They're built through deliberate, repeated choices. Repeat the steps outlined here and continue to choose the next fire you want to address. Over time, you'll have designed systems and procedures to delegate responsibility and measure performance for the tasks that you delegate.

WHY THIS MATTERS

The chaotic morning described earlier was an important moment for our organization, not because nothing went wrong, but because, despite what went wrong, the business absorbed every disruption and kept moving forward even without my input.

This tool exists to help leaders begin building that same resilience, not by stepping away prematurely, but by building something strong enough to step back from that will continue to thrive one thoughtful decision and planned system at a time.

Shelly Schoff is the owner of Crabtown Cleaning, a locally owned residential cleaning company serving Anne Arundel County, Maryland. With a deep belief that leadership is first and foremost about people, Shelly has built a values-driven business focused on service, growth, and genuine care for both her clients and her team members.

Over the past decade, Shelly has helped Crabtown Cleaning grow into a trusted community presence by prioritizing culture, consistency, and meaningful relationships. She is especially passionate about developing systems that support frontline employees, mentoring leaders, and creating a work environment where people feel seen, supported, and equipped to succeed.

Beyond business, Shelly is deeply committed to giving back to her community through partnerships, service initiatives, and donating time to nonprofit programs such as Cleaning For A Reason. Her work and leadership reflect a simple belief: when you take great care of people, everything else falls in place.

Connect with Shelly:

Email: shelly@crabtowncleaning.com

Website: https://www.crabtowncleaning.com

Facebook: https://www.Facebook.com/crabtowncleaning

Instagram: https://www.Instagram.com/crabtowncleaning

Learn More About Cleaning For A Reason:
https://cleaningforareason.org

CHAPTER 19

MACK TRUCK THEORY: BECAUSE PAYROLL CANNOT WAIT

TRANSFORMING EMERGENCIES INTO SUSTAINABLE OUTCOMES

Sabina May

MY STORY

"I have to go. I know we're in the middle of processing payroll, but I just got off the phone with my doctor. It's cancer. I can't talk now, but I need to hand off my workload."

It's the worst-case scenario we all fear. Many clients scramble, then call in panic to ask how soon we can begin. The fear that employees won't be paid keeps me up at night and has driven me to reassess everything payroll-related.

Years ago, we rolled out one of those personality assessments to my team. My number one strength was Restorative: People who are adept at dealing with problems, figuring out what's wrong, and resolving them. When I read it, I immediately thought: *That sums me up to a T!* From a color-coded closet so I don't have to think about what to wear when I'm rushing out the door, to a categorized pantry so I don't search for an ingredient, I always look for a more efficient way to do things.

While on a cruise with my husband, I analyzed the job-costing methodologies used on the ship before a show began. My focus on operational efficiency is constant; I cannot stop evaluating micro and macro elements in every situation.

"I just got off the phone with the school. My daughter is being taken to the hospital. I don't know when I'll be back. Here is everything my replacement will need while I am out."

These were my words to my boss, almost 25 years ago. I incorporated the Mack-Truck theory into my work long before I knew what it was. The quote I started the chapter with is from a team member to me, years later, after we standardized the practice in my company, PaySpecs.

At this point, you may be asking, "What is the Mack-Truck theory and how does it apply to me?" The premise is simple: If I were hit by a Mack truck tomorrow, could someone pick up exactly where I left off and do what I do? Now apply that principle to every person in your department, including payroll. Over the years, I've been asked to make the question a little less tragic. I prefer to think that if someone wins the lottery, they will provide the grace of a transition before leaving.

From a PaySpecs perspective, the Mack-Truck theory is that no one person should be indispensable because of the knowledge they hold; rather, because of the skills they possess. It means asking, "Is it transparent and is it sustainable" in every aspect of our work. As a single mom, I always had a contingency plan in place. When leaving our kids with family while my husband and I enjoyed a weekend getaway, it was about printing detailed instructions with friends' numbers, the best take-out restaurants, their favorite playgrounds, and who to reach in an emergency. It's having a fireproof box in the cabinet by the door with the most important documents.

The day I received the call from the school, I provided my boss with a checklist I had created and maintained for each of my 20 clients, along with all supporting documentation. It took less than 15 minutes to transition them to another implementation rep. When I created PaySpecs, I knew this was the foundation I had to build upon.

Last week, a Chief Talent Officer sent an email to her HR/Payroll team with whom we are partnering: "This process exposed the majority (if not all) of our vulnerabilities and process issues. If you don't know a problem, it is hard to fix it. Now we know the majority of them have a strong partner in PaySpecs who will help us implement process improvements in a transparent and sustainable way. Sabina's favorite words!"

I talk about these concepts so often that my clients quote them! It is the bedrock of PaySpecs and is at the very core of the Mack-Truck Theory. Applying them allows our clients to avoid preventable emergencies, navigate planned transitions and unavoidable shifts, and support employees in being less stressed and more efficient.

Throughout my young adult years and in the early days of PaySpecs, my entrepreneurial grandfather would press me for a detailed six-month, two-year, and five-year plan. He insisted on knowing my how, not just my goals. Our talks frequently returned to sustainability: "What if things go wrong?" "What's your contingency for your contingency?" These questions pushed me to think deeper about "What would happen if?" I also ruminated on something I read: "Companies can become outdated because they refuse to adapt to new technologies and processes, clinging to old ways even when they're no longer successful."

But how can you adapt if you don't know what's wrong? How can I plan for a backup plan if I can't imagine what could break along the way?

I've worked with many clients whose payroll administrators are worn down from working long hours with restless employees they're trying to support, and are crumbling under the weight of the responsibilities they feel. They work nights and weekends, forgoing vacation days, waking at the crack of dawn to confirm their employees were paid on time. It's just not sustainable. It's extremely difficult to keep running at a marathon pace when payroll is incorrect or burdensome every pay period. It's equally exhausting for administrators to chase down employees and managers or to continually play catch-up. Data integrity is lost when systems do not communicate as they should, leading not only to more manual entries (potentially increasing errors) but also to incomplete system integration.

Emergency situations quickly highlight the holes in processes and systems. I often tell my team and clients this, usually when we're knee-deep in payroll catastrophes. The moments expose processes that don't follow policies, incorrect data reporting, compliance issues, Band-Aid solutions for employee needs, or hidden system breakdowns. Even when problems are identified, our experience shows they are fixed with patched solutions rather than a holistic approach.

It's not surprising that so many clients wait until the breakdown to find the vulnerabilities. After all, I started PaySpecs for this specific reason: There was the HR director at a charter school who had to push back the payroll implementation start date multiple times, including once because she was also the head cheerleading coach, and one of her students had broken an arm. There was the time I got an earful from the irate boss because he wanted to know where the complete incompetence resided within his department.

Payroll staff are often over-allocated and/or under-trained for the responsibilities they hold: Frequently, management isn't even aware of the breakdowns because administrators work feverishly behind the scenes to ensure employees' pay is correct. My heart is always heavy when I walk into these scenarios. I know we can fix them quickly, but it pains me to see how desperate the situation has become by the time they reach out.

I love it when clients proactively bring us in to review system functionality, data integrity, third-party feeds, and administrative procedures. We regularly start by analyzing employee payroll and HR questions and investigating why they occur. By addressing the root causes, we can quickly resolve issues for several employees at once. Similarly, shadowing their payrolls for one pay period emphasizes the process inefficiencies and how unsustainable the current methodologies may be. There's nothing better than seeing a team and their systems finally working effectively!

Earlier, I mentioned that the Mack-Truck theory can help us avoid preventable emergencies. I'd argue that almost all payroll crises we encounter or detect are avoidable:

- Employees not receiving pay on pay date
- Improper calculation of overtime or non-exempt employees' pay
- Hunting down late timesheets (often with the same repeat offenders). Insert eye roll here.
- Last-minute changes from Finance, HR, or management. How many times have we seen annual bonuses, open enrollment changes, or merit increases that we knew about two months ago, submitted the day before, or while processing payroll?
- Payroll admins walking out without notice or due to illness.
- Amended W2s
- Failed audits
- Ghost employees
- Credit card, deduction, overtime, and timesheet fraud
- General Ledgers with incorrect payroll journal postings
- HR, payroll, retirement, benefits, and other disparate systems not matching employee or payroll data

I get heart palpitations every time I think about each of these client scenarios! I can picture the faces and the systems, as if they were yesterday. I sat across from the processors' desk, shadowing a payroll, when, as she removed a manager's approval, and overwrote an employee's timesheet, she happily exclaimed "I drove in with her today! I know she started much earlier than these hours show," it never crossing her mind that her friend may have been sitting in the cafeteria or catching up on personal emails before logging in for the day. We're frequently brought in because of a known payroll crisis, but the one that tops the cake was the employee who left 1,200 W-2s, unstamped, at the post office on January 31 and declared she had no intention of returning to the office. And then there's the client whose Labor Administrator had fraudulently added a minor deduction to all 600+ employees, wrote himself a check every payroll (using an alias), accounted for it through Accounts Payable, and then deleted all deductions six weeks before he resigned, 18 months after the fraud began.

Antiquated systems are another area I regularly see neglected. I know it's easier to keep the status quo, especially when they appear to be functioning, but it's been masked by the administrators, not out of mal-intent but because they care. They want what's best for their employees, so they regularly find a workaround to keep things moving. I always think of ducks treading hard underwater but appearing so calm above the water.

While I was in implementation, and in the 23 years since, one of my favorite sayings was "Garbage in—Garbage out," meaning that if the data wasn't clean before implementation began, it's not going to magically correct itself in a new system. Systems often aren't maintained either because management believes they are working or because they don't have the resources to support them. But the biggest reason I see is that payroll just hasn't kept up with the times.

When I started out in implementation, the client payroll system was housed on a single, password-protected CPU in a locked office. Someone had to be physically present in the facility and push a button, or people wouldn't get paid. We loaded a CD onto the client's computer and used printed manuals to guide us in setting up their systems.

Man, I am old! I once joked with someone that I used to have "Time-Life operator headphones," which prompted me to explain what "Time-Life" was, why they had "operators," and why I was tethered to my machine, all while I felt myself aging by the moment. *Sigh*. I digress.

The payroll preview function was just released. Just a year prior, reviewing payroll before final submittal wasn't a thing. Seriously! In implementation, they'd hit the submit button, cross their fingers or say a prayer, and wait until the next day to discover if the client's payroll was correct. In those 25 years since, payroll preview moved from implementation-only to as many times as we please, and the payroll system transitioned from that CPU to a company server with in-house programming to the internet platforms of today. Our verifications shifted from reviewing hundreds or thousands of sheets of paper, often side by side with a colleague while we called out names and numbers, to systems that automatically calculate net-to-net variances. As automation has advanced, I often tell payroll admins they can finally conduct the analyses and run the reports they want, rather than rely on manual entries. With AI projected to generate many of our processes within the next seven years, our role will again shift to oversight and compliance.

When we started out as a virtual company, people thought I was crazy. "But when will you get an office?! When you have 20 employees? 40?"

My answer has remained: "Never. No need. I never again want to work full-time in an office setting. Everything can be accomplished virtually, through transparent communication."

"But how will you communicate and get work done? Where will files reside? Please tell me not on the Cloud!"

15 years later, the pandemic hit, and everyone finally understood how we could function without a brick-and-mortar location. But with the world working from home, processes changed again.

I knew 20 years ago, in part because of the pressing questions from my grandfather, that the key to sustainability is letting go of processes and systems that are no longer effective, being willing to modify them over time, and routinely evaluating day-to-day with a fresh lens. As I tell my team and clients, "I don't care if it's the first time in 18 years we're discovering this hole in our process. We're going to ensure it never occurs again by finding the long-term solution."

If you're following the exact same process with the exact same, unmodified systems put in place more than five years ago, it's probably time to revisit the process and/or systems. I suspect my sister is also hearing my dad's voice tell the same story we've heard on repeat since we were young kids, about the perils of his client who refused to change.

To maintain sustainability, our tools, processes, and communication must be transparent. How many of those previously mentioned scenarios could've been avoided if management knew what was really happening within their payroll department, or the potential long-term savings if they were permanently fixed? What if it's an easy, small shift to change the entire payroll processing perspective?

Back in the day (remember, I've been doing this a long time), our payroll departments had paper files that accumulated in their "Payroll Inbox" file folder, which sat in the corner of their desks throughout the pay period until processing day. They put their heads down and processed for two or three days until they hit that submit button. I still see processors doing this today, only with digital files. Instead of these grueling processes, we can make a slight course adjustment to ease the burden of continually playing catch-up to a proactive payroll approach. I call it "Shovel while snowing." During a snowstorm, my husband and I will shovel an inch or two at a time, so we don't break our backs digging ourselves out of a 24-inch snowfall. Similarly, our method is to tackle a little bit of payroll each day by setting a firm deadline and communicating the need to all departments. Processing day should be about scrubbing data instead of entering it.

Lastly, implement tools and documentations available to all necessary parties. We've all worked with that person who just doesn't want to share information. Sometimes, it stems from the disillusionment with job security. Other times, it's a lack of time or personnel to cross-train. In all scenarios, they leave, taking their knowledge with them.

In our early years of PaySpecs, we did what most companies do. We had a single processor, a backup in case of emergency, and our project folks. We quickly learned why the standard process eventually falters: when one person does much of the work, they become blind to the process and documentation. The backup person, in turn, is not prepared to process payroll proficiently, leading to errors and eroding both systems and policies.

To be clear (notice the pun), transparency isn't about visibility. I'm chuckling as I recall a client, a nationally known company, whose offices were glass walls with glass desks so the owner could see exactly what was being done at any moment. Ironically, that very same CEO was unaware of the intentional fraud taking place under his watch. We found that we must involve multiple people to maintain the efficiencies we implement, and that, to do so effectively, our documentation and tools must not only be accessible to all but also written in a way that anyone can follow. Working in a silo doesn't work for long-term sustainability in payroll.

While I once deemed my continual need for change a weakness, "Why can't I just be content with what is?" I am now extremely grateful for the willingness to continually evaluate and adapt as needed. I am proud to tell people we were beta testers for Microsoft 365, and that we've created processes and tools that have sustained and evolved over the years to best support our team and our clients. I'm aware of the uniqueness of being a small business for as many years as we have, based solely on our reputation. I love that my team has long-term seniority, in part because we, too, operate by the Mack-Truck Theory, which allows flexibility and support within our PaySpecs family, especially in times of need.

THE TOOL

Ask these Mack-Truck Theory questions about yourself and each team member at your company:

1. Do our policies match our procedures, or have our procedures overshadowed our policies?

2. If something happened to me today, could someone pick up where I left off with no communication?

3. Are my procedures documented? How and where are they accessible? Are they written in a way that someone who has never looked at your systems or completed your tasks could follow?

4. At the start of every week and each day, ask:

    a. What fires need to be put out? (My goal is always "none")

    b. What embers are simmering and can turn into a fire soon if not addressed immediately?

    c. What could spark if not addressed sooner rather than later?

Once you start applying these principles, you'll quickly find that the Mack Truck Theory is not just a payroll best practice; Transparency and sustainability can transform every aspect of your day-to-day being. I hope you'll find yourself asking these questions as you continue to find ways to ease your mental load and navigate life more meaningfully and efficiently.

Sabina May has been the owner and president of PaySpecs, LLC, a 100% referral-based, fully virtual company, for 20 years. From inception, PaySpecs has remained vendor-neutral and does not partner with any third-party company, so every recommendation is made with the client's best interest in mind.

With a gentle nudge from her husband, Sabina created PaySpecs, leveraging her implementation background to address the need for client-side support. Sabina quickly transitioned to solving payroll emergencies and providing long-term co-sourced payroll solutions. Whether it's supporting a payroll department of one or an HR team of ten, Sabina and her team demonstrate their commitment to clients facing compliance or staffing challenges. PaySpecs serves clients across all industries, from biotech and nonprofits to government contractors, unions, schools, and manufacturing, in both the public and private sectors, applying a standard, adaptable methodology customized to any platform, using time-proven, dynamic tools and processes for clients ranging from 2 to 2,000+ employees.

PaySpecs helps minimize disruptive events by ensuring continuous review of regulatory updates, maintaining transparent documentation, cross-training teams for redundancy, and regularly integrating feedback from process and data reviews. By championing a structured yet flexible operational framework, PaySpecs greatly reduces fires and adds stability to its clients.

The name PaySpecs is a tribute to Sabina's mother, who owned TeleSpecs, a market research firm specializing in telephone research, surveying nationally recognized brands and products. She taught her daughters that glass ceilings were meant to be broken by being a female business owner in the 1970s and '80s.

When not photographing her son at his hockey games, Sabina enjoys exploring the world with family, laughing with friends at game night, or rejuvenating at live music or theater events. She also values family times gathered around the kitchen with her adult daughters and granddaughter.

Connect with Sabina:

Email: smay@payspecs.com

Website: http://www.payspecs.com/

LinkedIn: http://www.linkedin.com/in/sabina-grandin-may-08b5a4/

CHAPTER 20

RENOVATING A CENTURY-OLD BUSINESS

GROWTH AND MODERNIZATION WHILE MAINTAINING CORE VALUES

Rick Miller

"You need to buy the business from your parents."

Joe, a mentor and friend, suggested I reverse course on my plan to sell my fourth-generation family business to another company, which I believed would be the solution to my current headaches.

Buy out my parents? Could I even afford to do that?

And why would I want to?

My mind raced, turning over the merits of a suggestion I somehow never considered.

"You've put a lot of hard work into building this business, Rick," he told me. "You should be the one who benefits from that."

He had a point.

The last decade was the business equivalent of being shot out of a cannon. Since joining Zeskind's ten years prior, I grew gross revenue at the business my great-grandfather started by over 500 percent. I oversaw the construction of a new warehouse, developed a sales team, started a door manufacturing facility, instituted an ERP system, tripled the staff and truck fleet, hired a general manager, and became a 50% owner with my parents.

To an outsider looking in, I was a successful fourth-generation business owner. But for the last few years, I continuously put out fires, struggled with employee issues, and needed to be everywhere at once. I was the company's top salesperson, but also the only one who could negotiate a real estate contract—or a cell phone contract, for that matter. Furthermore, my parents and I invested significantly in the company, and the price of rapid growth had their stress levels through the roof.

A serious offer to buy the business came in, and I saw it as an easy off-ramp. But what Joe suggested got me thinking about what I accomplished and what still needed to be done.

Our company is missing clear long-term goals. We lack timely and accurate financial statements, so we can't do any serious annual budgeting. We have no set policies and procedures, and no way to let potential customers know what products we offer.

If I were allowed to take 100% control of our business, addressing these new concerns would be my new responsibility. For the past ten years, I had focused solely on growth and what I believed were important renovations. I knew I had to fundamentally change my relationship with my business if I were to lead this company through its 100th year of existence and beyond.

I looked back up at Joe, shocked by the audacity of what he just said. He gave me a reassuring nod.

"Don't worry, Rick, I'll introduce you to my banker. He'll tell us if he can make this work."

* * *

For the previous 83 years, Zeskind's Hardware operated out of a rowhome corner store in Baltimore. Customers walked up to a small counter surrounded by floor-to-ceiling wooden shelves filled with decades of tools, lightbulbs, paint cans, plumbing supplies, and more. Most items were hidden behind the counter in thousands of wooden cubbies and tiny drawers. Each customer was helped one-on-one with their hardware needs.

My great-grandfather, Sam Zeskind, opened the store in 1925, and my dad started working for his grandfather as a teenager in the 1960s. My parents purchased the tired little store from Sam in 1973, and they grew it into an incredibly successful small business.

At 13, I started working there alongside the other two employees, doing screen and glass repair and stocking shelves. As a teenager, I once helped a customer find replacement lightbulbs and wiper blades for a Ford Model T that had been buried in a drawer for half a century. When the customer asked the price, he was shocked when my dad answered, "Whatever it says on the box." They were each marked 25 cents, and that customer went home happy.

For decades, we used handwritten receipts and three-piece carbon charge tickets for account customers. The pricing of each item, current inventory levels, and the location of every item in the business were all safely stored inside my dad's head.

My mom was the CFO, head of HR, and did all the critical, important things to keep the business running smoothly. Accounts payable, accounts receivable, licenses, collections, insurance, and much, much more.

Even after earning my college degree and landing my first "real job," I still went in on Saturdays when my dad needed help. I knew he wanted me to follow in his footsteps, and although hardware was clearly in my DNA, working ten-hour days, six days a week behind the counter at the little corner store was not.

My mind changed, however, after several grueling years in construction project management and a few more in international building product sales. I saw an opportunity to bring what I learned to grow the family business in my own way, and decided to leap. At 28 years old, I left my corporate career and joined Zeskind's full-time. I was engaged, with a wedding in June and hoping to start a family soon after. I was full of optimism about the job that lay ahead of me as I joined the business my family had run unchanged for nearly 100 years.

So here I was, ten years later, contemplating yet another step in Zeskind's growth.

If I take Joe's advice and become the sole owner, I want to maintain all the "character" of the old business. If I expand, I have to bring my mindset and the operations forward into the current century—without losing the authenticity and one-on-one service that generations before me made a cornerstone of Zeskind's.

Spoiler alert: Joe's banker came through. A year after that initial discussion, I completed an internal family buyout of the remaining half of the business. The intensity of that process was transformative, and helped me realize how much longer my renovation project would take.

Now, 18 years into my journey as a fourth-generation business owner, I'd like to share five key things that helped me transform a legacy business into a thriving modern enterprise. Here we go.

THE TOOL

SEEK OUT MENTORS

Of all the things you should be doing, the very first one, and the one you will continue doing, is to seek out mentors. These are the people who have seen it all and been through the battles you might be facing. They're going to provide perspectives you never would've imagined and share the distilled knowledge of decades of succeeding in business.

For instance, when Joe heard I was considering a serious offer to sell our fourth-generation business to an outside investor, he reached out.

"Don't make the mistake I did, Rick. I can't believe I missed the opportunity to buy my own family's business," Joe lamented.

He was the President and CEO of one of our key vendors, and he didn't want me to make the same mistake. This level of sharing knowledge and experience can only come from mentors.

There are some really amazing, insightful, and intelligent people out there who love to share what they've learned. There has to be mutual respect, which is how you know it's a good fit. And as a mentee, you have an obligation to take what is being taught and do great things. I've found mentors to be generous people who are typically very successful and aren't looking for compensation. They want to empower other business owners to grow, hire more people, find success, and be positive contributors to society.

THE FRACTIONAL EXPERTS

I wish I had known about fractional experts sooner. Fractional chief financial officers, fractional human resources consultants, and fractional marketing professionals can each bring their skills to your business without being full-time employees. These are super mentors who can adapt to various situations. As a small to medium-sized business owner, fractional experts give you top-tier advice, quick action on difficult challenges, and are true partners on call as needed.

Finding the right fractional expert for your business is not always easy. We currently have three in the roles of CFO, HR consultant, and Marketing Coordinator, and I'll share how they help my company.

Our fractional CFO, Brian, works directly with our full-time controller every month to ensure the goal of having our completed financials by the 15th of each month. Brian is also our CPA, but he also offers CPA and fractional CFO services to other clients. This is perfect, as we would never have enough work for him to do full-time at our company.

HR issues can get really serious, really fast. While the normal day-to-day HR and payroll type issues are fairly monotonous, there are often HR flare-ups that require someone on your team who understands the rulebook and can instantly extinguish the flames. Enter Susan, our fractional HR consultant and leadership coach. Susan is an HR superhero, able to calmly and thoughtfully assess even the most implausible situations with employees. Susan provides a calm and clear assessment of the situation and gives expert-level options for resolution. On top of that, I personally trust her as my business coach, and she helps my team grow through her leadership training programs.

Marketing needs for companies can vary widely. A national competitor of mine might have a gigantic budget for lead generation and promotions through a variety of channels, while a small local company like ours lacks those generous resources. Our fractional marketing coordinator, Christine, understands the needs of our business and quickly manages and executes marketing projects for us. She oversees website design, works with graphic designers to create event banners and signage, and ensures that our social media messaging stays on point and consistent.

TIMELY AND ACCURATE FINANCIAL REVIEW

Your fractional CFO will tell you how having accurate financial statements is critical to driving your business forward. This is how your team will make good business decisions.

Getting this information quickly is key, so set a goal for when your monthly financials will be completed, then enforce policies and procedures that ensure this happens consistently. For us, it took 18 months to reach our goal of preparing the previous month's financial review within two weeks of the month's end, and we haven't missed a review session in the last four years.

This wasn't possible in the past because we didn't have a CFO dedicated to our company. Brian shares our core values and walks us through our financial bill of health each month. He is someone with expertise that our controller can reach out to for difficult general ledger-related questions.

As a result, we can act quickly on issues, spot payroll spikes, identify drops in monthly gross margin, catch concerning trends in accounts receivable, and understand the true cost of the debt we have incurred. It also helps us identify wins, such as record months of sales and margins, highest-performing salespeople, best-paying customers, and paint a picture of our ideal customer and our perfect vendor. The financials serve as a divining rod for the strongest growth opportunities in our company.

I love collecting our financials every four weeks after each monthly meeting, dropping them into the folder for that year, and being proud that no matter what the bottom line reads that month, we consistently accomplish that goal.

KNOWING WHAT YOUR BUSINESS IS WORTH AND WHY

I'm just going to say it—as a business owner, one of the most important things you need to understand is the value of your business—at all times. You need to know how to calculate the value of your business, and set goals for valuation even as far out as your planned exit date. You pour your life into this thing, risking everything you have, and most likely signing personal guarantees with vendors, leaseholders, and banks. You should know what you have.

You may have investments, 401(k)s, whatever. These are pocket change compared to the investment that is your company. As a business owner, you have a unique opportunity to take this one crazy thing known as your business and make it infinitely more valuable than all your other investments.

Many business owners don't think about the value of their business and never plan an exit strategy, at least not until it's too late, when they finally find out what makes a company valuable and that they missed the mark. For a vast majority of small and medium-sized businesses, it comes down to good financial records, how well the owner delegated to trusted employees, and how well the repeatable systems and processes are implemented. As business owners, learning to trust our team with running our business can be one of the most difficult tasks, but also one of the most valuable assets we create.

Almost always, a business valuation is based on a multiplier called Earnings Before Interest, Taxes, Depreciation, and Amortization, or EBITDA, which can be found on your profit and loss statement. An EBITDA multiplier in the upper range is indicative of a self-running business that is not reliant on the owner's day-to-day involvement, connections, and sales prowess. Most likely, a company that sells for a high multiple of EBITDA has sparkling clean financials, great employee morale, and processes and procedures so impressive that a buyer wants to implement them to improve their existing operations.

I'm not here to get into specifics about calculating and using EBITDA to value your business, but I am here to say that you *must* understand this concept and take the time—which may likely be years—to work with your CFO on accurate financials. The results can mean the difference between giving away millions of dollars in value and having millions more for your retirement.

Your financials will tell one story, which will be the baseline for the negotiation. Those are indisputable numbers you've achieved, and it's critical to have them well-documented. There are infinite ways to construct a deal for the sale of a company. Is the buyer purchasing your corporation, or just your assets? Is real estate involved? What are the terms, the interest rate? Will the seller hold part of the note? Will there be performance incentives or tranches, and is this a structured buyout? Do you understand the tax implications of all of these options, both on your side and the buyer's side, for negotiation purposes?

If you've listened to your mentors, assembled your fractional superheroes, and delegated to your amazing team to create timely financials, you're going to have an attractive and much more valuable business to sell in the future.

TUITION PAYMENTS—ALWAYS LEARNING

Zeskind's General Manager, Greg, has been a mentor of mine for more than two decades. I worked for him when I first started in the millwork industry, and he has always been a great friend. When we learn a costly lesson or are required to hire an expensive expert beyond our normal scope, Greg and I call it "tuition."

The first time we needed to sign a complicated lease, I paid a lawyer $400 an hour to walk me line by line so I knew what we were signing. By the end, I knew every inch of that 60-page lease, and I finally felt like I knew what I was getting myself into. For the next lease, and the one after that, I handled most of the review myself and sent a fraction of the redlines back over to the lawyer for his final review, which cost nothing compared to the first one. The first one was tuition.

Other tuition payments are more indirect. A costly mistake made by a team member exposes holes in your employee training. Changing the name of an acquired business teaches you the value of loyal name recognition. Leasing a delivery truck when you could've saved in the end by buying one prepares you for making a better decision next time. It's all tuition.

And sometimes you feel like you're paying for your Ph.D. For instance, we thought using a national payroll company would save us time and money as our business outgrew our in-house capabilities. We quickly learned how difficult it was to solve problems, both simple and large, within such a large corporation, but it took four years to uncover hidden costs we unknowingly incurred for years. Those were never mentioned during the sales pitch.

* * *

These are five of the most critical pieces of advice I have for legacy business owners working to modernize. Some concepts came easily during my business renovation, but others are clearer in hindsight.

Since I first began my journey 18 years ago, I've achieved this internal family buyout, plus two purchases of similar-sized family-owned businesses. All three transactions were incredibly different, but each deal required the input of new mentors, professional advice from fractional experts, good financials on both sides, a clear understanding of the value of my business and the business we were buying, and the extensive knowledge gained through tuition.

Even if you're not acquiring a business or renovating an old one, planning ahead and using these tools from the beginning will make your business stronger and more valuable.

Rick Miller is the President and owner of Zeskind's Hardware & Millwork, a manufacturer and wholesale distributor of doors, windows, trim, and other custom-made items. With 25 years in the building materials and construction industry, Rick has worked for homebuilders, building material suppliers, and manufacturers throughout his career. In 2008, he started as the fourth generation at Zeskind's and has never looked back. Here is a link to the company's 100-year timeline: https://zeskinds.com/about-us/

Creating a manufacturing facility from scratch, Rick was able to control quality and provide a finished product second to none, coming from Zeskind's shops. A focus on historic tax credit projects formed the basis for Zeskind's business in Baltimore City, and these types of projects were a personal passion of Rick. Advocating for historic buildings and ensuring they retained their character while fighting for the use of an energy-efficient building envelope was challenging, but this led to working directly with officials at the city, state, and federal levels of historic preservation, as well as collaborating with major window manufacturers' engineering teams. You can check out all of Zeskind's catalogs and vendor partners here: https://zeskinds.com/resources/

While historic buildings were a core business, Rick also grew Zeskind's manufacturing to support larger-format projects, supplying new-construction homebuilders and multifamily projects with a new level of service and passion.

Outside the business world, Rick spends time with his wife and two children at their 1830's farmhouse and small farmette, including chickens, and hopes to expand into goats and donkeys one day. He's a car enthusiast and visits Cars & Coffee whenever possible. He and his wife, Joni, love frequenting restaurants in downtown Annapolis, Maryland, and spending time around the Chesapeake Bay with family and friends.

Connect with Rick:

Website: https://www.Zeskinds.com

LinkedIn: https://www.linkedin.com/in/rick-miller-84a4476/

Facebook: https://www.facebook.com/Zeskinds

Instagram: https://www.instagram.com/zeskinds_hardware

YouTube: https://www.youtube.com/@rickmiller7689

Connect with Rick's Fractional Experts:

Strategic HR: Susan Mahaffee, People Rise: https://www.peoplerisellc.com/

CPA/Fractional CFO: Brian Chrest, Chrest CPA: brian@chrestcpa.com

Marketing: Christine Hickey, Severnside Marketing: https://www.severnsidemarketingmd.com/

CHAPTER 21

STOP STEALING FROM YOUR LEGACY

HOW ONE DECISION TODAY SECURES GENERATIONS TOMORROW

Maura Dowd Sniegoski

MY STORY

"Unfortunately, we are unable to approve your client for the product applied for. Our decision was due to a recent diagnosis of…"

I received that email in response to my own child's life insurance application. He was three years old. And in the language of underwriting, he was now *uninsurable*.

I remember staring at the screen, rereading the words as if they might rearrange themselves into something kinder.

This can't be real, I thought. *He's a toddler. He hasn't even started kindergarten. How can a life that's barely begun already be labeled too risky?*

Just days earlier, my oldest child had been approved, barely weeks ahead of a diagnosis that would've closed that same door forever.

Weeks.

I remember thinking, *what if I had waited? What if I had told myself I had more time?*

Two children. Two different outcomes. The difference between them wasn't love or preparation.

It was timing.

That moment reshaped everything I thought I knew about protection. Life insurance isn't about predicting death. It's about protecting possibility. It's about acting while the door is still open.

Most people believe they have time. I learned that "someday" is not a strategy, it's a gamble. And that lesson didn't just change how I parent. That lesson changed how I see every business owner who sits across from me. They build something meaningful and assume there will be a later.

Because what you're building, your income, your company, your team, your family's future, depends on the same fragile truth I learned that day:

The opportunity to protect what matters does not stay open forever.

I became a life insurance broker out of necessity.

At the time, my children navigated significant medical challenges. They needed me home and needed consistency. Our family still needed income. I searched for work flexible enough for hospital visits and therapy appointments. I wanted to provide financially without leaving them behind.

How do I stay present and still provide? I remember wondering.

How do I build a future when everything feels uncertain?

But I also wanted the work to *matter*. If I were going to build something in the middle of uncertainty, I wanted it to have a real impact on the families I served. I wanted work that meant something on the hardest days, not just the easy ones.

That's how I found this profession. And three of the very first policies I ever wrote were on my own children. That decision wasn't symbolic; it was strategic.

I chose policies to serve them into adulthood. These would guarantee their insurability, no matter their future health. I already knew how quickly things can change.

When my oldest was approved just weeks before his diagnosis, I felt relief and a kind of quiet terror.

That could have been him, I thought. *That could have been another door closing.*

When my middle child was denied, the lesson became permanent. A single diagnosis, one that will follow him forever, closed a door I hadn't even realized could lock.

This isn't fair. He's a child. How can one word on a chart decide his future?

That was my first, most personal lesson in this business: Waiting feels responsible, until it becomes irreversible.

I didn't insure my children because I expected to lose them. I insured them because I refuse to let their futures be dictated by a diagnosis they never chose.

And once you learn how fast a door can close, you stop assuming it will always be open.

Most people don't avoid life insurance because they are careless. They avoid it because they are busy and building, always in motion, with the urgent outrunning the important.

Entrepreneurs are especially wired this way. You leap before you feel ready, trust yourself to figure it out, solve problems in real time, and take risks others won't.

That instinct builds companies. But the same instinct can quietly end them.

We normalize risk in the name of resilience. We tell ourselves:

I'm healthy.

I'm in my prime.

I'll get to it later.

Once the business is bigger...

When things settle down...

We convince ourselves that protection comes after we've arrived, but life doesn't wait for your next quarter.

And delay doesn't just create vulnerability; it creates *an inheritance of chaos*. Because when protection is missing, the cost of that delay is never paid by the person who postponed it. It's paid by the people they love.

I've sat across from spouses who lost partners. They then lost businesses.

I've seen parents lose income before they had time to grieve.

I've seen employees arrive at work to find the doors closed. Not because tragedy is common. But because preparation is rare. And the absence of a plan turns one loss into many.

What I learned through my own family's experience, and through hundreds of conversations since, is this:

Protection isn't pessimism. It's leadership. It's the willingness to say, *What I am building matters enough to protect*. It's the courage to look beyond the present moment and decide that the future deserves continuity.

That belief is what separates intention from legacy.

In the next section, we'll zoom out from my story and into yours, into what it truly means to be a business owner, a provider, a builder of systems that reach far beyond yourself. We'll explore why every entrepreneur is already shaping a legacy, whether they realize it or not. And why one decision can be the difference between what ends with you and what endures because of you.

BUSINESS OWNERS AS LEGACY BUILDERS

If you own a business, you're a legacy builder, whether you've ever used that term or not. You're building more than revenue. You're building:

- Stability for your family
- Opportunity for your employees
- Value for your clients
- Momentum that extends beyond you

Your business is not just a job. It is an ecosystem.

It feeds households.

It pays mortgages.

It funds college accounts.

It gives people identity and purpose.

Even the smallest business touches more lives than most owners realize. And yet, most entrepreneurs insure everything *except themselves*.

We insure our buildings, our vehicles, our equipment, our data, and our inventory. We protect what we can see. But we often leave the most valuable asset uninsured: The human being on whom everything depends. The one who carries the vision. The one who signs the checks. The one who holds the relationships. The one whose presence keeps the entire system moving.

You.

I can almost hear the quiet pushback.

This feels dramatic.

This doesn't apply to me.

I'm in my prime.

I'll handle this later.

I used to believe "later" was a plan too, until I learned how quickly a door can close.

Life insurance has been framed as something morbid; something you buy because you're afraid. But that framing misses the truth entirely.

Life insurance is not about planning for death.

It's about protecting *momentum*. It's the difference between:

- A spouse having *options* instead of ultimatums.
- Employees having *stability* instead of shock.
- A business having *breathing room* instead of a fire sale.
- A family having *time* instead of panic.

It ensures that:

- A partner isn't forced to sell in grief.
- A team isn't suddenly unemployed.
- A business doesn't die just because a person did.
- A family doesn't trade dreams for survival.

Legacy isn't what you build. It's what survives you. And survival doesn't happen by accident.

Entrepreneurs adapt, pivot, recover, and believe in their ability to figure it out, so we assume our families will, too.

My spouse will manage.

My team will land somewhere.

The business will work itself out.

But what those thoughts really say is:

I hope my loved ones are strong enough to carry what I didn't prepare.

Grief is not a strategic planning environment. Shock does not lend itself to wise decision-making. And without liquidity, without immediate, accessible capital, options disappear fast. Businesses don't fail because people stop caring. They fail because they run out of time.

Rent is still due. Payroll still matters. Vendors still expect payment. Mortgages don't pause for heartbreak. Without a plan, survival becomes a race against reality.

I've watched capable, intelligent, motivated people lose everything not because they lacked skill, but because they lacked runway. And a runway is exactly what life insurance provides. It's not a morbid payout. It's a continuity fund. It buys:

- Time to breathe
- Space to grieve
- Margin to decide
- Power to choose

It allows a family to say: *We don't have to decide this today.*

It allows a business to say: *We can stabilize before we restructure.*

It allows a spouse to say: *I don't have to dismantle what we built just to survive.*

That isn't fear-driven. That is foresight.

The most dangerous myth in small business is this:

I'll take care of it later. Later feels responsible. Later feels practical. Later feels like adulthood. But later is a moving target. Later becomes the next quarter. Next quarter becomes next year. Next year becomes "after things calm down." And things never calm down when you're building something meaningful.

I learned with my own children that timing isn't neutral. Doors close. Health changes. Eligibility disappears. And once that happens, intention becomes irrelevant.

What you can do today may not be available tomorrow. Your insurability is a window. Your affordability is a season. Your leverage is temporary. The best time to protect your legacy is not when everything is perfect. It's when the door is still open.

Every business owner already plans for the future. You think about:

- Scaling
- Hiring
- Systems
- Succession
- Exit strategies

You already understand that what you're building is bigger than this moment. Life insurance is simply the missing layer in that planning. It is the only tool that:

- Creates immediate liquidity.
- Transfers risk away from your family.
- Funds continuity at the exact moment it's needed.
- Works regardless of market conditions.

No loan does that. No savings account does that. No asset sale does that. It's not an expense. It's infrastructure. It's the financial equivalent of a foundation. And like any foundation, it doesn't draw attention until it's missing.

In the next section, I'll give you a simple, practical framework you can use to evaluate your own risk and responsibility as a business owner.

It's called the **L.E.G.A.C.Y. Framework**—and it will help you quantify what continuity actually costs, who it protects, and what kind of leader you choose to be.

THE TOOL

THE L.E.G.A.C.Y. FRAMEWORK AND YOUR NEXT DECISION

Clarity creates action.

Not fear.

Not pressure.

Not guilt.

Clarity.

That's why I use the **L.E.G.A.C.Y. Framework**, because legacy isn't what you *intend* to leave behind. It's what actually remains when you are no longer in the room.

This is not about morbid thinking.

It's about responsible leadership.

Read each step slowly. Let yourself answer honestly.

L — LOSS POINT

WHAT WOULD IMMEDIATELY STOP IF I WASN'T HERE?

Think beyond income.

Who signs the checks?

Who holds the client relationships?

Who makes the decisions when something breaks?

Who carries the vision?

Ask yourself quietly:

If I'm honest, how much of this only works because I'm here?

Your loss point reveals how dependent your ecosystem is on you. It's not a weakness. It's a reality. And reality is where leadership begins.

E — EXPOSED PEOPLE
WHO WOULD FEEL THE IMPACT FIRST?

Your spouse.

Your children.

Your employees.

Your partners.

Your clients.

Pause here.

Who would be forced into urgent decisions they never asked for?

Who would carry consequences they didn't create?

These are the people your leadership already protects every day. This framework simply asks whether that protection extends beyond your presence.

G — GAP OF TIME
HOW LONG COULD THINGS REALISTICALLY CONTINUE WITHOUT YOU?

Not in theory. Not in hope. In reality.

- 30 Days
- 90 Days
- 6 Months
- A year

How long could:

- Bills to be paid?
- Will payroll be met?
- Does the business remain functional?
- Will your family remain financially stable?

Ask yourself:

Would thirty days even be enough?

This step isn't about fear. It's about the runway.

A — AMOUNT NEEDED

WHAT WOULD IT COST TO KEEP EVERYTHING ALIVE LONG ENOUGH TO STABILIZE?

Add it up:

- Mortgage or rent
- Household expenses
- Business overhead
- Payroll
- Debt obligations
- Transition costs

This number represents *continuity*. Not luxury. Not excess. Stability.

What does "breathing room" actually cost in real dollars? That number is not morbid. It's merciful.

C — CONTINUITY PLAN

WHAT SYSTEM IS ALREADY IN PLACE TO FUND THAT AMOUNT INSTANTLY?

Be honest.

Is it savings?

Would assets need to be sold?

Would debt be required?

Would the business be dismantled?

Or…is there nothing?

Ask yourself: *If this happened tomorrow, what would they really do?*

A plan that requires grief-driven liquidation is not a plan. Continuity requires liquidity. And only one tool is designed to deliver it at exactly the moment it's needed.

Y — YOUR DECISION
AM I WILLING TO LEAVE THIS TO CHANCE, OR WILL I DECIDE WHAT HAPPENS NEXT?

This is the only step no one else can complete for you.

You already know:

- What you're building
- Who depends on you
- What's at stake

The question is not *whether* there is risk. The question is who will carry it.

Am I willing to let timing write this story?

Or am I ready to lead beyond myself?

The number you uncover through this process is not a death benefit. It's a **legacy preservation fund**. It's the bridge between chaos and continuity. Between collapse and choice. Between *"We lost everything"* and *"We survived this."*

You don't buy life insurance because you expect to die. You buy it because you expect what you've built to matter. Because you believe your family deserves options. Because your employees deserve stability. Because your work deserves the chance to outlive a single moment, a single illness, a single unforeseen turn.

I insured my children not because I expect to lose them, but because I refuse to let their futures be dictated by something outside their control.

That same principle applies to you. Protection is not pessimism. It's leadership. It's the decision to say: *What I am building matters enough to protect.*

If this chapter stirred something in you, if you felt both the weight of responsibility and the possibility of peace, that's clarity asking for action.

The L.E.G.A.C.Y. Framework will show you *what* to protect.

A professional can help you decide *how*.

If you're ready to stop leaving your legacy to chance, I invite you to reach out to me. Not for a policy. For a conversation.

One that honors:

- What you've built
- Who you're building it for
- And the future you intend to leave behind

Because legacy isn't accidental. It is designed.

And one decision today can ensure that what you're building now continues to matter for generations tomorrow.

Maura Dowd Sniegoski is the CEO of Sniegoski Life Group, which is dedicated to empowering clients and building a network of female leaders in the industry. With a deep commitment to personalized service, Maura focuses on understanding each client's unique needs and providing tailored solutions that ensure financial security and peace of mind.

As a visionary leader, she is passionate about mentoring and supporting women in insurance and all industries, fostering a dynamic agency where female professionals thrive. Whether you are planning for the future or navigating complex policies, Maura is here to guide you with expertise and empathy.

When Maura is out of the office, you will find her baking with her three children and husband, attending one of many kids' sporting events, dancing and reciting the lyrics to any '90s hip-hop or Taylor Swift song, or daydreaming about going back to her native New York for all the food.

Connect with Maura:

Website: https://www.sniegoskilifegroup.com

Instagram: https://www.instagram.com/maura.sniegoski/

LinkedIn:
http://www.linkedin.com/in/maura-dowd-sniegoski-6338778
https://www.linkedin.com/company/sniegoski-life-group

CHAPTER 22

INVESTING IN COMMUNITY LEADERSHIP

A PATH TO A PURPOSE-DRIVEN, MEANINGFUL LIFE

Kris Valerio Shock

MY STORY

"When you don't get cast, you volunteer."

My heart was broken, but those words guided me through some of the hardest transitions of my life.

When I was 12 years old, growing up in Annapolis, Maryland, the local community theater held auditions for a brand-new musical adaptation of Charles Dickens' A Christmas Carol. I convinced my best friend Susie to audition with me, telling her, "We're a shoo-in! My mom is good friends with the director!" Surely, we'd both get cast. Susie came with me, and we auditioned. Susie got cast in the plum role of Scrooge's younger sister, Fanny, and I did not get a part. I was crushed. It was then that my grandfather, one of the founders of the local community theater, told me, with no uncertain terms, "When you don't get cast, you volunteer."

As heartbroken as I was, I was smart enough to follow Pap-pap's advice, and when I showed up to volunteer, the head costumer entrusted me with the role of Costume Mistress. I assisted the head costumer in creating costumes for the wide array of cast members. Still, more importantly, once the play opened, it was my responsibility to attend to any immediate needs throughout the production, including sewing on buttons and mending torn garments, placing the chains on the ghost of Jacob Marley, and other duties as assigned. It was a truly marvelous experience. I developed a deep sense of connection with the performers and the stage crew. *So, this is what it feels like to be part of something bigger than myself!*

When, several years later, it was time to declare my major in college, after many experiences on stage in school and community plays, we all assumed I'd be a theatre major. I was born into a creative family. My dad was a book designer by trade, though his first love was classical portrait painting. My mom acted in local productions, earned her MFA in acting when I was a teenager, later wrote, directed, and produced local theater, and then taught drama at a private school. My oldest brother played the French horn; my next oldest brother helped my dad with his book design business and crafted beautiful calligraphy. So, while it's a cliché that when most actors break the news to their parents that they want to be an actor, their parents desperately try to convince them to choose a more conventional path, it was quite the opposite in my house.

I left for Towson University in Baltimore, Maryland, to major in Theatre, where I performed in Mainstage productions from my freshman year onward. In my final semester, I joined a study abroad program and spent my last six months of school in Leicester, England. Less than two months in, I received an urgent message to call home. My gut told me something was terribly wrong. The moment my dad picked up the phone,

"What? Who?" I asked. "It's Darin. He's gone." My middle brother had died in a car accident. My life is divided into before and after the loss, a story for another time. I flew home immediately to be with my family, then returned to England ten days later to finish the semester and graduate remotely from Towson.

Upon my return home that summer, I entered a new phase: the real grieving began, not in any dramatic way, but in the small, relentless moments of ordinary life continuing without my brother. Still working through the loss, I found I wasn't ready to head to New York or Los Angeles to begin my acting career. Instead, I decided to stay closer to home for a while, finding a measure of healing within my local community theater.

During this period of regrouping, I took a day job as a casting assistant at Central Casting in Washington, D.C., specializing in casting for industrial training films produced by government agencies and corporations, as well as extras for Hollywood films shot locally. Learning the business from the inside was invaluable. Still, I ultimately wanted to be an actor, not a casting assistant, so after a while, I decided to quit the job and pursue auditions in the Baltimore-Washington area. Booking a weeklong role on *America's Most Wanted* marked my entry into the professional actors' unions, a critical milestone. Securing my union cards gave me access to higher-level auditions and legitimate industry opportunities. With that credibility and eligibility in place, moving to New York was the logical next step.

I spent eight years working as an actor in New York. The actual acting work ranged from more industrial training films, loads of "extra" work filling in as background in movies including *Money Train, The First Wives Club,* and *The Mirror Has Two Faces,* and small roles in soap operas and TV shows, including *Sex and the City* and *Homicide: Life on the Street.*

I supported my acting work with a host of part-time gigs: casting assistant, event host, promotional model, bartender, waiter, teacher, Gymboree instructor, part-time nanny for the rich and famous, and more. Some years I was more of an actor, and some years more of a bartender and jack-of-all-trades.

While the goal was to book paid acting work, I remembered Pap-Pap's advice: "When you don't get cast, you volunteer." When the paid gigs were slow, I didn't wait to get cast; I self-produced to create work I was proud of and that agents and casting directors could see. *Close Encounters of the Human Kind* was a showcase I produced featuring 10 actors (including me) in 5 scenes. Then, in 2001, I was invited to participate in a monologue night where actors wrote and performed their own pieces. After doing a few of these events, I discovered a common theme among my characters. They all grappled with the balance between the speed and quality of their lives. A one-woman show called *Moving at the Speed of Life* emerged. I played 12 different characters, all managing the speed and quality of their lives.

The morning of 9/11, I flew out of Laguardia Airport on an American Airlines flight to California. I was in the air during the attacks on the World Trade Center. Returning to New York, I felt an even deeper connection to the city and its people, determined to rise above the tragedy. The workshop production of *Moving at the Speed of Life* opened in October 2001 in a small theater in Greenwich Village, just a month after 9/11.

While bringing the show to life and exploring the unintended consequences of living at the speed of life, I realized I loved the craft of acting but not the livelihood. This was a turning point. *I want to build a life of purpose and fulfillment in the real world.* In a pivotal conversation with my friend and producer Jane, I asked, "Will you feel resentful if in ten years, we're still self-producing our own work?" She replied without hesitation, "Absolutely not." Jane was in it for the long haul, but I instantly knew it was time for me to take a different path. After the workshop and limited runs of my one-woman show in New York and Maryland, I began looking for a job back in Annapolis.

The transition to a more conventional career presented new challenges. Deciding to move back to Annapolis was only the first step; figuring out how to make a living outside of acting was another. Reflecting on my experience selling myself as an actor, I thought sales might be a good fit. Since I had also worked in restaurants, a job posting for a wine sales rep seemed like a reasonable next step. A boutique wine distributor hired me to sell wine to retail and restaurant accounts in Washington, D.C. Early on, however, I realized the job was more about parking in D.C. (long before parking apps, it was all about the quarters) and navigating the city than it was about the wine. Nevertheless, I persevered for over a year, developing valuable skills I carry with me to this day.

While still working in wine sales, I began searching the local paper for other opportunities, wanting a career better aligned with my interests. I spotted a Membership Development role at the local Chamber of Commerce. At the time, I wasn't entirely sure what chambers of commerce did, but I sensed it might be a better fit. I was fortunate to be hired and soon discovered a love for connecting people to one another and to opportunities. The skills I had nurtured as an actor—understanding characters, objectives, and motivations—helped lay a strong foundation for my new role.

While serving as VP of Membership for the Annapolis & Anne Arundel County Chamber, I had the opportunity to participate in the Leadership Anne Arundel (LAA) community leadership program. Having grown up in the arts community and then moving away for the first decade of my professional life, I lacked a full understanding of the community we served. Going through the Leadership Anne Arundel Flagship program with a cohort of other community leaders gave me a 360-degree understanding of the community and a rich network of business and personal relationships that I cherish and nurture to this day.

One of the most memorable experiences of the program happened in the opening retreat. We were assigned a project in a small group. I don't recall what the assignment was, but I do recall the pit in my stomach. *What if I don't have the experience or knowledge to complete the project successfully?* I then learned the power of a diverse group of people, all bringing different skills to the table. In our small group, I only needed to bring my talents to bear, as the other members brought theirs. The project felt effortless and even fun. Relief washed over me. *I get it, I don't have to know everything. I just have to do what I do best.* The experience set the bar for future group collaboration in my leadership journey.

Following my experience at the Chamber, I had the opportunity to serve as Executive Director of the Chesapeake Regional Tech Council. It was in this role that I was invited to become the co-founder of Ignite Annapolis. If you're not familiar with Ignite events, they are like mini-TED talks. Speakers get five minutes and 20 slides that automatically advance every 15 seconds. The first Ignite Annapolis event was thrilling to produce, bringing together a diverse array of speakers for an evening of inspiration, community, and connection. At the time, my plate was full running a small nonprofit, and my co-founder had other priorities, so even though the event was a great success, we didn't have the capacity to make it a regular event.

After seven years at the Tech Council, it became clear it was time to move on to the next challenge in my leadership journey. I took a job as a Senior Business Development executive for a marketing firm. I took the job mainly because they offered great flexibility in the timing of my joining the firm, which meant I could wrap up my tenure at the Tech Council purposefully and set them up for a smooth transition following my departure. I was far more thoughtful about how the transition would serve the Tech Council than I was about whether I was truly a match for the job.

Within the first couple of weeks, I knew this was not the right match for me. It became clear I was moving away from something, not purposefully toward anything, and I began to calculate how long I had to stay in the role. *How long do I endure this before I start drifting too far from who I want to be?* The months went by, and while my work ethic and sheer determination supported my success in the role, I drifted further from a sense of purpose. It was a low point. About a year into my tenure with the firm, I realized I had to do something to get back into a zone where I felt purposeful. "If you don't get cast, you volunteer" evolved into "If your job isn't fulfilling, volunteer your talents to the community," I remembered the delight the Ignite Annapolis experience brought me, and I invited a dear colleague from the Tech Council to join me as lead organizer for an Ignite Annapolis event. Just as before, producing Ignite Annapolis brought a wave of community connection and sheer joy. The days flew by as I continued with the marketing firm by day and produced Ignite Annapolis in every spare moment. I then received a call from a former Tech Council member. "How would you like to serve as Senior Director of the Office of Strategic Industries and Entrepreneurship for the Maryland Department of Commerce?" It was an exciting new challenge with a start date immediately following the Ignite Annapolis event.

Once again, a volunteer opportunity that called on my passions and strengths made me feel alive, connected, purposeful, and productive. Showing up in life in this way led me to my next professional role.

My time at Commerce was an invaluable experience. Though I never planned to work in government, the role introduced me to relationships and opportunities beyond my expectations, and I continued producing Ignite Annapolis events during my tenure. When the Executive Director of Leadership Anne Arundel announced his retirement, the opportunity to have a direct impact on my hometown proved irresistible. I applied for the President & CEO role at Leadership Anne Arundel.

I began my new role in May of 2019, and as I was making my way through my first year, in March of 2020, COVID happened, and I went from learning the ropes of the nonprofit to helping it survive and thrive through the complexity of the pandemic. I discovered that LAA graduates were on the front lines of every facet of managing, surviving, and thriving despite the COVID crisis. They created food assistance programs, ran vaccination clinics, and managed PPP loan programs. *They were the helpers.*

Community leadership participation not only helps the community, but when the match is right (when it aligns with your talent and the community's needs), it drives personal fulfillment like nothing else.

When I went through the program, I felt how profoundly it served my need to understand my community at that point in my life. Serving on the staff side, I witness people embracing the experience in all different seasons of their lives—rising leaders to those transitioning to retirement and everywhere in between.

In my experience, "When you don't get cast, you volunteer" isn't altruistic; it's a direct pathway to connection and ultimately joy. Reflecting on my journey, I see the transformative power of community leadership. If you're looking for purpose, fulfillment, or stronger connections, I encourage you to get involved in your local community, whether through volunteering, joining a leadership program, or simply reaching out. Take the step; you'll be amazed by what you gain and how much you can give back.

THE TOOL

Finding a volunteer opportunity that truly aligns with your interests and strengths can be time-consuming and hard to navigate. Community Leadership Programs, such as Leadership Anne Arundel (LAA), make that journey faster and more fulfilling. They offer a welcoming, immersive way for community leaders of all ages to understand how a community truly works and to apply their talents, values, and skills to create lasting, positive impact.

Found in small, medium, and large communities across the country, most Community Leadership Programs offer a Flagship experience that spans approximately ten months. The journey typically begins with an Opening Retreat, concludes with a Closing Retreat, and includes a series of theme-based sessions in between. These sessions provide deep dives into critical sectors of the community, such as economic development, education, government, public safety, health, cultural arts, and more. Participants engage directly with community leaders, explore complex challenges, and examine how systems intersect. Through this structure, participants gain clarity not only about the community but also about their own purpose within it.

Organizations invest in Community Leadership Programs because the return extends far beyond professional development. Participants return with broader perspectives, stronger leadership skills, and deeper community awareness, helping organizations think more strategically and operate at higher levels. Exposure to diverse viewpoints sharpens decision-making, increases emotional intelligence, and helps leaders recognize personal biases. Participation also reflects a strong commitment to corporate social responsibility, signaling that an organization values both its people and the community it serves.

Individuals invest in Community Leadership Programs to expand their personal and professional networks while gaining insight into meaningful opportunities for engagement and service. The Flagship experience is often transformative, offering exposure to diverse perspectives, honest dialogue around tough leadership issues, and the chance to develop action-oriented solutions. Participants leave with a clearer sense of how they can align their careers, volunteerism, and leadership with their values.

Communities, in turn, benefit from a growing network of informed, connected, and committed leaders. Graduates emerge as advocates, volunteers, and changemakers equipped to help shape the future. In this way, Community Leadership Programs do more than develop leaders—they cultivate lives of purpose, connection, and meaningful impact.

Community leadership programs are typically based on a specific geography, so to find one near you, simply search for your city, county, or state, then add "community leadership program."

Learn More:

http://www.leadershipaa.org

https://igniteannapolis.com/

https://www.ignitetalks.io/

Kris Valerio Shock is the President & CEO of Leadership Anne Arundel, located in Annapolis, Maryland. As a graduate of the Leadership Anne Arundel Flagship program (2006), Kris is excited to mix her personal and professional experience to expand the visibility, value, and reach of the LAA program and network.

Before joining LAA, Kris served as the senior director of the Office of Strategic Industries and Entrepreneurship at the Maryland Department of Commerce, where she led a team of experts in manufacturing, education and innovation, agribusiness and energy, and entrepreneurship and capital attraction.

From 2008 to 2015, Kris served as executive director of the Chesapeake Regional Tech Council, overseeing its transition from a local group focused on Anne Arundel County to a regional business organization with members across the Washington-Annapolis-Baltimore region. Under her leadership, the tech council's membership grew from 200 to more than 300 companies, grant funding increased by more than 200 percent, and total revenue doubled. Shock also designed, developed, and implemented a marketing strategy to promote the council's new brand and ongoing program of work.

Kris has a Bachelor of Science from Towson University. A native of Annapolis, she is the Co-founder of Ignite Annapolis. Kris lives in Annapolis with her husband, three stepdaughters, her dogs, Lucy and Desi, and her cat, Mimi. Kris serves on the United Way of Central Maryland (UWCM) Region United Network (RUN) Advisory Board of Anne Arundel County and is a proud volunteer at the SPCA of Anne Arundel County.

Connect with Kris:

Website: https://www.leadershipaa.org/page/Team

LinkedIn: https://www.linkedin.com/in/krisvalerioshock/

AN INVITATION TO RISE

THIS BOOK IS AN INVITATION.

Maybe you found it because you know one of the co-authors—someone you trust, admire, or work alongside. Maybe one story caught your attention, and then another did. Maybe you recognized yourself in a chapter you didn't expect to read all the way through.

Or maybe you picked this up because you're a small business owner trying to figure out how to grow without losing your values. Maybe you're an HR professional who carries more responsibility than authority. Maybe you're a department leader—or the person who was *volun-told* to "handle the people stuff" because someone had to.

HOWEVER YOU ARRIVED HERE, YOU BELONG IN THIS CONVERSATION.

Every role has reach. Every seat carries influence. And every person—yes, even just one—has the ability to shape the experience of work for others in ways that last far longer than policies, handbooks, or org charts.

DON'T UNDERESTIMATE WHAT YOU CAN DO.

You don't need a title, a budget, or permission to be a memorable and impactful leader. You only need awareness—and the willingness to act on it. Use your platform, whatever it looks like today, to make things better. Better conversations. Better expectations. Better care for the people doing the work.

Because leadership isn't reserved for the loudest voice or the highest position. It shows up in moments—how you listen, how you respond, how you choose to lead when no one is watching.

As one of my favorite Maya Angelou reminders goes: *when you know better, you do better.*

This book offers knowledge, perspective, and shared experience. What you do with it is where the real work—and the real impact—begins.

WHEN PEOPLE RISE, EVERYTHING CHANGES.

ACKNOWLEDGEMENTS

This book exists because of trust—shared, offered, and returned.

To the co-authors of *When People Rise*: thank you for being early adopters of this vision and for trusting me with something deeply personal to all of us—our stories, our work, and our belief that workplaces can be better. This book is not about any one voice; it's about all of us, and the people we serve every day. It reflects why we do what we do and the shared commitment we have to bringing humanity, clarity, and care into the places where people spend so much of their lives.

To my mom, also Susan—my biggest literal cheerleader—thank you for your unwavering belief in me, even when the path wasn't clear. You've carried "Deddy's" love, determination, and courage with you since the moment you trusted him enough to leave Hungary and take a leap together. Though he is now an angel, his spirit lives on through you, and through the grit, heart, and perseverance you modeled for me every single day.

To my sister, Agnes, aka Sissy—once my "little" sister and now very much my big one in all the ways that matter: thank you for being the first to say yes. You put your own money behind this project and stood beside me without hesitation, simply saying, *"If you're doing it, I'm in."* You've been with me on this life journey, holding my hand through the hard moments, the brave moments, and everything in between. Sharing this book with you makes it even more meaningful.

To my son, Peter: I know you see me working a lot. My hope is that what you've watched isn't just effort, but purpose. That you use what you've seen as fuel for your own dreams, that you support others, stand alongside other women, and become part of a future generation of leaders who make a real difference in a world that still has so much brokenness—and so much possibility.

To my friends, colleagues, and the many connectors who believed in this vision and helped it grow: thank you for opening doors, making introductions, and expanding what was possible. To those who helped me find incredible voices—like Margie Hamner, whom I met at our authors' retreat just before the closing deadline—your generosity and belief in the power of connection made this project richer in ways I could never have planned.

To the people who have been in and out of my life for one reason or another: thank you. Each of you has shaped me, stretched me, and helped make me who I am today. I carry those lessons forward with gratitude.

To the Leading Lady community: thank you for embracing me so fully and for showing me what's possible when women truly support one another. Because of this community, I was introduced to our publisher, Laura Di Franco, and to the idea that impact expands when we rise together.

And to Laura and the entire Brave Healer world—this is something I never imagined I would do, or even dream of. Being part of this community, inspiring others, and being inspired in return by these co-authors is beyond comprehension. This experience has once again changed me, and I am endlessly grateful.

This book is proof of what happens when people trust, collaborate, and believe in themselves and in one another.

"Just like moons and like suns,
With the certainty of tides,
Just like hopes springing high,
Still I'll rise."

- Maya Angelou